Amigurumi
Animal Hats

20 Crocheted Animal Hat Patterns
for Babies and Children

Linda Wright

To my friends near and far with gratitude for enriching my life

Also by Linda Wright

Amigurumi Toilet Paper Covers

Toilet Paper Origami

Toilet Paper Origami On a Roll

Toilet Paper Crafts for Holidays and Special Occasions

Lindaloo Enterprises
P.O. Box 90135
Santa Barbara, California 93190
United States
sales@lindaloo.com

ISBN: 978-0-9800923-7-0
Library of Congress Control Number: 2014912970

Contents

Introduction

When I was working on a previous amigurumi book, *Amigurumi Toilet Paper Covers*, a 20-something friend who teaches preschoolers commented that my projects would make cute hats for children. I laughed at the prospect, but her suggestion stayed in the back of my mind. When a trip to visit my two great-nieces, aged 3 months and 3 years, was brewing, I decided to give it a try. I modified one of my patterns and made them each an owl hat. They were adorable—and even more so when the girls had them on. And so the seed for *Amigurumi Animal Hats* was planted. Old critters were reinvented and new ones created to result in this book of whimsical wearable amigurumi.

Amigurumi (ah•mee•goo•roo•mee) is a Japanese term for crocheted animals. It is cute, colorful, cartoonish—and a craze that brought fresh excitement into the world of crochet in the early 2000s. Amigurumi is done by crocheting in a continuous spiral using one primary stitch—the single crochet—which makes it easy to master. First and foremost, I love the look of single crochet, but it is also a tight stitch that works up into a nice, thick fabric for a warm and sturdy hat.

These patterns include variety that will teach you different techniques. Ears are made from crocheted circles or cylinders, pom poms or tassels; snouts are stuffed or flat; and eyes are crocheted or cut from felt. Eventually you may wish to mix and match components to create your own unique creatures. Four hats of special merit to me are the dog, made in the likeness of my pet, Maggie; the chicken, in memory of my grandfather's poultry farm; the monster, inspired by my son's many monster drawings; and the snow leopard, commemorating my son's favorite stuffed animal, now well-worn and stored as a keepsake.

I am happy to share my collection of amigurumi animal hat patterns. May they bring smiles and cozy moments to many!

General Directions

If you're new to crocheting, or if you need to brush up, the following pages include instructional diagrams for the stitches used in this book.

If you like to learn by watching, YouTube.com is a treasure trove of excellent crocheting tutorials. To find what you need, just search on the stitch you want to learn and, for the best results, include "crochet" in your search. For example, magic ring crochet (also known as the magic circle or magic loop), single crochet, or loop stitch crochet. Several embroidery stitches are used for finishing touches on the hats and these can also be found demonstrated on YouTube, for example, chain stitch embroidery and the French knot.

For a hand-picked source of tutorials, I have assembled a collection of my favorites on Pinterest. You can view them at www.pinterest.com/LindalooEnt/ on boards named "Amigurumi Tutorials" and "Embroidery Tutorials". There you can watch demonstrations for all of the stitches and techniques needed to make amigurumi animal hats.

Amigurumi is meant to be crocheted rather tightly. This will prevent fiberfill from showing through your stitches on any stuffed pieces. Be sure to check your gauge at the beginning of each pattern.

This book uses U.S. crochet terms. If an instruction says sc, that is a U.S. single crochet—or a U.K. double crochet. Please refer to the stitch diagrams on the following pages to be sure you are making the stitches as intended.

Hat Sizing

This book contains hat patterns in three sizes: Small (newborn - 6 months), Medium (6 months - 18 months), and Large (18 months - 5 years). Children's head sizes can vary widely within age groups, so, if possible, the best way to determine hat size is by measuring the child's head circumference and then selecting the size that most closely matches.

To measure a head's circumference, place a tape measure across the forehead, just above the ears, and measure over the hair around the full circumference of the head. Hold the measuring tape firmly, but not too tightly.

A finished hat's circumference is approximately 1 inch smaller than the head circumference because crocheted fabric stretches and this allows for a snug fit. Some people like a looser fit, so take personal preference into consideration when choosing a size.

Size	Age	Head Circumference	Hat Circumference
Small	Newborn - 6 mo.	14-15"	13-14"
Medium	6 mo. - 18 mo.	16-17"	15-16"
Large	18 mo. - 5 yrs.	18-19"	17-18"

Any hat can be made larger or smaller without altering the pattern by using a larger or smaller crochet hook.

Essentials

Yarn

All of the yarn used to make amigurumi animal hats, except for the lion's mane, is worsted-weight yarn marked as number 4. Look on the label for the yarn weight symbol containing a 4 in the middle of a ball of yarn. Choose a soft yarn for a nice, soft hat. Soft yarns frequently include "soft" in their name. I primarily use Caron "Simply Soft". Other yarns that I like include Red Heart "Soft Yarn", Lion Brand "Vanna's Choice" and Lion Brand "Cotton-Ease". A yarn that is made of acrylic fibers, or acrylic blended with cotton or wool, is an ideal choice because the hat will be colorfast, washable and hold its shape well. The yarns that I used for these patterns are listed in the Resources section at the back of the book.

Scissors

You will need a small pair of sharp scissors.

Crochet Hook

All of these patterns have been designed for a U.S. H/8 (5 mm) crochet hook. You may need to go up or down a hook size to obtain the gauge, or, as I mentioned previously, if you just want to make a hat larger or smaller. My absolute favorite hook is the Clover Soft Touch Crochet Hook (pictured below, center). I love the ergonomic grip which keeps my hand from going numb when crocheting for long periods of time and the shape of the head which inserts easily into a stitch.

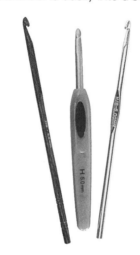

Yarn Needle

Yarn needles, or jumbo tapestry needles, have a large eye and a blunt point. They are made from metal or plastic. You will use one to sew the various pieces of your hat together and also to finish it off by weaving the loose ends into your work.

Stitch Markers

Stitch markers are used to keep track of where a round of crochet begins and ends. You can use a safety pin, bobby pin, paper clip or purchased stitch markers. I recommend the locking stitch markers that are shaped like safety pins. They are very easy, secure and convenient to use. Making the correct number of stitches is important, so count to double check if ever you're not sure.

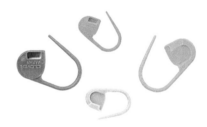

Polyester Fiberfill

Some of the small animal hat features, such as snouts or bulgy eyes, are stuffed with polyester fiberfill. This can be purchased by the bag at craft stores. One bag will go a long way!

Other Supplies

Disappearing Ink Marking Pen

This terrific marking tool is a felt-tipped pen with ink (usually purple) that disappears in a day or so. Purchase it at a fabric store, craft store or online.

Removable Notes

Use sticky notes to keep track of your place in a pattern. Every time you complete a round or a row, move the note down to reveal the next line of instructions. I wouldn't work without one!

Row Counter

Well worth the investment, a row counter keeps track of what round of the pattern you are crocheting. A pencil and paper can also be used.

Sewing Needle & Thread

You will need these sewing box basics when felt eyes are used.

Straight Pins

Use standard dressmaker's pins or long corsage pins to hold pieces in place before sewing.

Ruler

For measuring and marking.

Polyester Felt

When felt is used for animal hat eyes, it should be polyester. Polyester cuts cleanly with no fraying, sews easily, is washable and colorfast. (See Resources, page 81.)

Scotch Removable Double Sided Tape

Cutting small felt eyes can be tricky, but this product, used with the circle templates at the back of the book, makes it easy. Adhere template to felt with removable double sided tape. Cut around template using small scissors and cutting slowly. Remove template from felt.

Hole Punch

Holes are punched in paper templates for my connect-the-dots method of marking your work. Use a single-hole hand punch or even a kitchen skewer.

Arch Punch

If you will be cutting circles of felt for animal hat features on a regular basis, this tool is a handy aid. To cut felt with an Arch Punch, protect your work surface with a cutting board. Place a scrap of corrugated cardboard on top of the cutting board and then the felt. Hold felt steady with one hand and swivel punch with the other hand while applying gentle pressure. Continue swiveling clockwise — and then counterclockwise — until the cut is made. (For purchase information, see Resources, page 81, or check ebay.)

Toilet Paper Roll

This household essential makes a convenient hat form. Place hats on a TP roll to mark the placement of auxiliary features.

Crochet Stitches

SLIP KNOT

This is used to make a starting loop on the crochet hook.

1. Make a loop about 5 inches from end of yarn. Insert hook in loop and hook onto supply yarn (yarn coming from ball) at A.

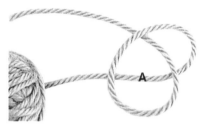

2. Pull yarn through loop.

3. Pull yarn ends to tighten loop around hook.

CHAIN (CH)

Start with a slip knot on hook.

1. Bring yarn over hook from back to front. Catch yarn with hook and pull it through the loop . . .

to look like this. One ch is done.

SINGLE CROCHET (SC)

This simple stitch is the primary stitch for amigurumi.

1. Insert hook in designated stitch. Note: Put hook under both loops that form v-shape at top of stitch unless otherwise instructed.

2. Yarn over and pull up a loop.

You will now have 2 loops on the hook.

3. Yarn over and pull yarn through both loops on hook.

4. You now have 1 loop on hook and the sc stitch is done.

LOOP STITCH (LP ST)

The Loop Stitch is a variation of single crochet. The loops will form on the wrong side of the fabric (the side opposite the side you are facing). When the Loop Stitch is used for a hat, you will turn it wrong side out when done. That way the loops will be on the outside—where you want them.

1. Insert hook in designated stitch, just as you do for a single crochet.

2. Wrap yarn around index finger of your yarn-holding hand to make a loop and lay loop on top of hook. Pull strands A and B through stitch C.

3. Yarn over and pull through all 3 loops on hook—A, B, and C.

4. The lp st is done.

SLIP STITCH (SL ST)

1. Insert hook in stitch. Yarn over and pull through stitch and through loop on hook (A and B).

2. The sl st is done.

SINGLE CROCHET DECREASE (SC2TOG)

The instruction "sc2tog" means to use single crochet to join 2 stitches together. It is a way to decrease or make the item smaller.

1. Insert hook in stitch, yarn over and pull up a loop . . . to look like this.

2. Insert hook in next stitch, yarn over and pull up a loop . . . to look like this.

3. Yarn over and pull through all 3 loops on hook . . . to look like this. The sc2tog is done.

Techniques

★ MAGIC RING

Most all of my amigurumi begins with the magic ring. This is the way to get a nice, neat center when crocheting in the round. The magic ring is an adjustable loop that you can tighten—like magic! It's not difficult—and well worth it. (An alternative to the magic ring, if desired, is to chain 2. Then begin Round 1 by working into the 2nd chain from the hook instead of the ring.)

1. Make a ring a few inches from end of yarn. Grasp ring between thumb and index finger where the join makes an X. Insert hook in ring, hook onto supply yarn at Y and pull up a loop . . .

to look like this.

2. Chain 1 . . .

to look like this. This chain does not count as a stitch.

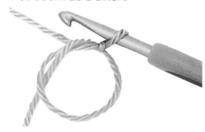

3. Insert hook into ring so you're crocheting over ring and yarn tail. Pull up a loop to begin your first single crochet . . .

and complete the single crochet.

4. Continue to crochet over ring and yarn tail for the specified number of single crochets for the 1st round.

5. Pull tail to close up ring. To begin the 2nd round, insert hook in 1st stitch of 1st round (see arrow).

BEGIN 2ND RND HERE

WORKING IN THE ROUND

Working in the round means crocheting in a continuous spiral. Most amigurumi is worked in this manner.

USING STITCH MARKERS

It can be tricky to keep track of your place when working in the round, so be sure to use a stitch marker. The pattern will remind you! Place the stitch marker in the first stitch of a round—after completing the stitch. When you've crocheted all the way around, remove the stitch marker, make the next stitch, and replace the marker in the stitch just made. This will be the first stitch of the next round.

WORKING IN LOOPS

When a single crochet (sc) stitch is made, you will see 2 loops in a v-shape at the top of the stitch. To crochet the patterns in this book, insert your hook under **both loops**. Patterns that you encounter elsewhere may indicate to crochet in the "front loops only" or the "back loops only" for a different effect.

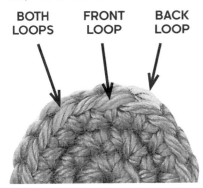

BOTH LOOPS   FRONT LOOP   BACK LOOP

CHANGING COLORS

To change color while single crocheting, work last stitch of old color to last yarn over, yarn over with new color and pull through both loops on hook to complete the stitch.

FASTENING OFF

This is the way to finish a piece so that it won't unravel. When you're done crocheting, cut the yarn and leave a tail. Wrap the tail over your hook and pull it all the way through the last loop left on your hook. Pull the tail tight and it will make a knot.

SMOOTHING THE EDGE

When fastening off, the knot can make a small bump in the edge of your work so that, for example, a round shape will not look as round as it should. To make the edge smooth, thread the long tail in a yarn needle and insert the needle down through the center "V" of the next stitch. This little step makes a big difference.

FRINGE

1. Follow pattern instructions for length and quantity of yarn strands to be used. Put hook through desired stitch, catch strand(s) in the middle and pull part way through stitch to make a loop. (Photos below show fringe being made with 2 yarn strands.)

2. With hook in loop, lay yarn ends over hook.

3. Pull yarn ends all the way through loop to make a Lark's Head knot. Take hold of ends and pull tight.

EYES

The eyes for the animals in these patterns are made from crocheted circles or circles of felt. The formula for a basic crocheted eye is simple: make a Magic Ring, then single crochet over the ring for the desired number of stitches and pull the ring tight. (See Magic Ring, page 12). The more stitches you work over the ring, the larger the eye. I use stitch quantities ranging anywhere from 4 to 10 stitches. Knowing the method, you can freely change eye sizes if you wish to create different personalities. When eyes are made from felt, it is important to cut a smooth circle. Work slowly and use small, sharp scissors. It is common to use buttons for the eyes of amigurumi; however, buttons are not recommended for items given to children under the age of 3. (Dislodged buttons present a choking hazard.) If your hat is for an older child, you may want to give button eyes a try. Two stacked buttons in graduated sizes are especially cute!

STUFFING

The goal in stuffing is to stuff firmly without stretching the crochet stitches. Pull a chunk of fiberfill from the package and gently work it into your crocheted piece. For these hats, you will only be stuffing small auxiliary features such as snouts. First, stuff the piece lightly, just until it holds its shape. Then, when you are almost done sewing the piece into position on the hat, pause to pack in more stuffing before sewing the final stitches. It is helpful to use a chopstick, skewer or eraser end of a pencil to push the final bits of fiberfill into place.

COUNTING ROUNDS

Periodically, it is good to count your rounds to ensure your place in a pattern. Fortunately, rounds are clearly defined and counting is easy. Each round makes a ridge. A groove separates the rounds. You need only to count the ridges. Take a look at the photo below to see that the circle has 5 rounds.

ASSEMBLING

The assembly stage of amigurumi hatmaking is an exciting time. This is when all pieces are sewn together and the project blossoms in cuteness! Thread a yarn needle with the long tail of your auxiliary piece (eye, ear, etc.) and use a whip stitch or running stitch to sew it to the hat. It's good to temporarily pin your pieces in place beforehand to decide where you like them the best. When the feature pieces are stuffed with fiberfill, I like to outline their placement first. This ensures that their shape stays true. For this purpose, templates are provided at the back of the book. You will find custom templates for several patterns and a selection of circles that will accommodate any piece with a circular end. Pin the template to the hat in the location that you like, then trace around it with a disappearing ink marking pen. Remove the template and hold your piece against the outline to sew it in place.

WEAVING IN ENDS

The final assembly instruction for every pattern is to weave in the ends. This is the way to hide and secure all of your straggly yarn tails. Thread the yarn end into a yarn needle, then skim through the back of the stitches on the wrong side of your work. Continue for about 2 inches, then turn and double back to lock the yarn into place. Trim the end close. When you turn your work to the right side, you should not see the woven ends. They should be tucked into the middle of your crocheted fabric.

POM POMS

Follow pattern instructions to wrap yarn around cardboard. Slide bundle off cardboard, tie in the middle and cut loops.

Fluff into a ball and trim into a nice round shape.

CLEANING

If you have used washable yarn, your hat will be easy to clean. Follow the laundry care instructions on the yarn label and wash as directed. The instructions are usually provided as universal care symbols. To interpret their meaning, see Yarn Care Symbols, page 84.

Embroidery Stitches

STRAIGHT STITCH

A simple, single stitch. Come up from wrong side of fabric at A and go down at B.

A   B

RUNNING STITCH

The Running Stitch is formed by a detached series of Straight Stitches. Make it by running the needle up and down the fabric at a regular distance. Come up at A, down at B, up at C, down at D, up at E, down at F, etc.

A   B   C   D   E   F

FRENCH KNOT

Bring needle up from wrong side at A. Place needle close to fabric and wrap yarn around needle 3 times. Push needle down at a point near A.

CHAIN STITCH

1. Bring needle up from wrong side at A. Put needle back in at A and out at B, but don't pull the needle completely through.

B

A

2. Wrap yarn around needle from left to right to form a loop.

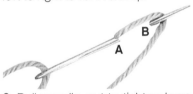

3. Pull needle out to tighten loop. First stitch is done.

4. Put needle in at B, and out at C. Repeat Steps 2 and 3 to complete 2nd stitch. Continue to make as many stitches as needed.

How to Read a Pattern

The following abbreviations are used:

st	stitch
ch	chain
sc	single crochet
sl st	slip stitch
lp st	loop stitch
rnd	round
sc2tog	single crochet decrease
* *	repeat
( )	stitch count

Each round or row is written on a new line. Most rounds have a repeated section of instructions that are written between two asterisks *like this*. The instruction between the asterisks is to be repeated as many times as indicated before you move on to the next step. At the end of a round, the total number of stitches to be made in that round is indicated in parentheses (like this).

Let's look at a round from a hat:

> **Rnd 6:** *sc in next 4 sts, 2 sc in next st* 6 times (36 sts).

This means:

Rnd 6	This is the 6th round of the pattern.
sc in next 4 sts	Make 1 single crochet stitch in each of the next 4 stitches
2 sc in next st	Make 2 single crochet stitches, both in the same stitch
6 times	Repeat everything between * and * 6 times.
(36 sts)	The round will have a total of 36 stitches.

So, following the instructions for Round 6, you will:

single crochet in the next 4 sts, 2 sc in the next st,

single crochet in the next 4 sts, 2 sc in the next st,

single crochet in the next 4 sts, 2 sc in the next st,

single crochet in the next 4 sts, 2 sc in the next st,

single crochet in the next 4 sts, 2 sc in the next st,

single crochet in the next 4 sts, 2 sc in the next st,

for a total of 36 stitches.

How to Measure your Gauge

Gauge is written as follows:

7 rnds of sc = 3" diameter circle

This means that when you've crocheted the first 7 rounds of single crochet on a piece, the circle (or hexagon) you've created should have a 3" diameter. So, when you have crocheted the first 7 founds of a hat, measure it. If your measurement is 3" (or even within 1/8") your hat will conform with the Hat Sizing Chart on page 7. To alter your gauge, adjust your crochet tension (tightness) or change to a larger or smaller crochet hook. It is very common for gauge to vary from person to person.

Owl

SUPPLIES

Worsted weight yarn in purple (approx. 45 yards) and green (approx. 55 yards) plus small amount of turquoise, white, black and yellow.

Size H/8 (5 mm) crochet hook or size needed to obtain gauge

Stitch marker

Yarn needle

GAUGE

7 rnds of sc = 3" diameter circle

HAT

With green yarn, make a magic ring, ch 1.

Rnd 1: 6 sc in ring, pull ring closed tight (6 sts).

Rnd 2: 2 sc in each st around. Place marker for beginning of rnd and move marker up as each rnd is completed (12 sts).

Rnd 3: *sc in next st, 2 sc in next st* 6 times (18 sts).

Rnd 4: *sc in next 2 sts, 2 sc in next st* 6 times (24 sts).

Rnd 5: *sc in next 3 sts, 2 sc in next st* 6 times (30 sts).

Rnd 6: *sc in next 4 sts, 2 sc in next st* 6 times (36 sts).

Rnd 7: *sc in next 5 sts, 2 sc in next st* 6 times (42 sts).

Rnd 8: *sc in next 6 sts, 2 sc in next st* 6 times (48 sts).

Rnd 9: *sc in next 7 sts, 2 sc in next st* 6 times (54 sts).

• FOR SIZE SMALL:

Rnds 10-18: sc in each st around; change to purple yarn in last st.

Rnds 19-27: sc in each st around. Fasten off.

• FOR SIZE MEDIUM:

Rnd 10: *sc in next 8 sts, 2 sc in next st* 6 times (60 sts).

Rnds 11-20: sc in each st around; change to purple yarn in last st.

Rnds 21-30: sc in each st around. Fasten off.

• FOR SIZE LARGE:

Rnd 10: *sc in next 8 sts, 2 sc in next st* 6 times (60 sts).

Rnd 11: *sc in next 9 sts, 2 sc in next st* 6 times (66 sts).

Rnds 12-22 : sc in each st around; change to purple yarn in last st.

Rnds 23-33: sc in each st around. Fasten off.

INNER EYE (MAKE 2)

With black yarn, make a magic ring, ch 1.

Rnd 1: 6 sc in ring, pull ring closed tight (6 sts).

Sl st in next st. Fasten off with long tail.

OUTER EYE (MAKE 2)

With white yarn, make a magic ring, ch 1.

Rnd 1: 6 sc in ring, pull ring closed tight (6 sts).

Rnd 2: 2 sc in each st around. Place marker for beginning of rnd and move marker up as each rnd is completed (12 sts).

Rnd 3: *sc in next st, 2 sc in next st* 6 times (18 sts).

Rnd 4: *2 sc in next st, sc in next 2 sts* 6 times (24 sts).

Sl st in next st. Fasten off with long tail.

EYE RIM (MAKE 2)

With turquoise yarn, make a magic ring, ch 1.

Rnd 1: 6 sc in ring, pull ring closed tight (6 sts).

Rnd 2: 2 sc in each st around. Place marker for beginning of rnd and move marker up as each rnd is completed (12 sts).

Rnd 3: *sc in next st, 2 sc in next st* 6 times (18 sts).

Rnd 4: *2 sc in next st, sc in next 2 sts* 6 times (24 sts).

Rnd 5: *sc in next 3 sts, 2 sc in next st* 6 times (30 sts).

Sl st in next st. Fasten off with long tail.

BEAK

With yellow yarn, ch 7.

Row 1: starting in 2nd ch from hook, sc2tog, sc in next 2 sts, sc2tog (4 sts).

Row 2: ch 1, turn, sc2tog twice (2 sts).

Row 3: ch 1, turn, sc2tog (1 st).

Fasten off with long tail.

EAR (MAKE 2)

Cut two 6-inch strands of green yarn and two 6-inch strands of purple yarn. Lay strands together and attach to one side of Hat using Fringe technique (see page 13). Trim to 1 inch. Repeat on other side of Hat.

ASSEMBLY

Sew Inner Eyes to Outer Eyes. Sew Outer Eyes to Eye Rims. Sew Eyes and Beak to Hat. Weave in ends. ♦

Cat

SUPPLIES

Worsted weight yarn in light gray (approx. 50 yards) and medium gray (approx. 50 yards) plus small amount of white, pink, and black

Size H/8 (5 mm) crochet hook or size needed to obtain gauge

Stitch marker

Yarn needle

GAUGE

7 rnds of sc = 3" diameter circle

HAT

The hat is worked by alternating 2 rnds of medium gray with 2 rnds of light gray. Change to alternate color in last st of every other rnd.

With medium gray yarn, make a magic ring, ch 1.

Rnd 1: 6 sc in ring, pull ring closed tight (6 sts).

Rnd 2: 2 sc in each st around. Place marker for beginning of rnd and move marker up as each rnd is completed (12 sts).

Rnd 3: *sc in next st, 2 sc in next st* 6 times (18 sts).

Rnd 4: *sc in next 2 sts, 2 sc in next st* 6 times (24 sts).

Rnd 5: *sc in next 3 sts, 2 sc in next st* 6 times (30 sts).

Rnd 6: *sc in next 4 sts, 2 sc in next st* 6 times (36 sts).

Rnd 7: *sc in next 5 sts, 2 sc in next st* 6 times (42 sts).

Rnd 8: *sc in next 6 sts, 2 sc in next st* 6 times (48 sts).

Rnd 9: *sc in next 7 sts, 2 sc in next st* 6 times (54 sts).

• FOR SIZE SMALL:

Rnds 10-27: sc in each st around. Fasten off.

• FOR SIZE MEDIUM:

Rnd 10: *sc in next 8 sts, 2 sc in next st* 6 times (60 sts).

Rnds 11-30: sc in each st around. Fasten off.

• FOR SIZE LARGE:

Rnd 10: *sc in next 8 sts, 2 sc in next st* 6 times (60 sts).

Rnd 11: *sc in next 9 sts, 2 sc in next st* 6 times (66 sts).

Rnds 12-33: sc in each st around. Fasten off.

EAR (MAKE 2)

Make 1 ear piece with pink yarn and 1 ear piece with medium gray yarn.

With pink or gray yarn, chain 7 loosely.

Row 1: sc in 2nd chain from hook and each ch across (6 sts).

Rows 2-3: ch 1, turn, sc in each st across (6 sts).

Row 4: ch 1, turn, sc2tog, sc in next 2 sts, sc2tog (4 sts).

Row 5: ch 1, turn, sc in each st across (4 sts).

Row 6: ch 1, turn, sc2tog twice (2 sts).

Row 7: ch 1, turn, sc in each st across (2 sts).

Row 8: ch 1, turn, sc2tog (1 st).

Fasten off. Weave in ends, weaving over any holes made by decreases.

Place pink and gray pieces wrong sides together. With gray yarn, sc pieces together along outer edge making 3 sts at each corner. Fasten off with long tail.

EYE (MAKE 2)

With black yarn, make a magic ring, ch 1.

Rnd 1: 6 sc in ring, pull ring closed tight (6 sts).

Sl st in next st. Fasten off with long tail.

NOSE

With pink yarn, make a magic ring, ch 1.

Rnd 1: 4 sc in ring, pull ring closed tight (4 sts).

SI st in next st. Fasten off with long tail.

SNOUT

With white yarn, make a magic ring, ch 1.

Rnd 1: 6 sc in ring, pull ring closed tight (6 sts).

Rnd 2: 2 sc in each st around. Place marker for beginning of rnd and move marker up as each rnd is completed (12 sts).

Rnd 3: *sc in next st, 2 sc in next st* 6 times (18 sts).

Rnd 4: *2 sc in next st, sc in next 2 sts* 6 times (24 sts).

SI st in next st. Fasten off with long tail.

ASSEMBLY

Sew Ears to Hat. Sew Nose to Snout. With pink yarn, embroider straight stitch mouth (see diagram) on Snout. Pull left and right sides of Snout gently to make a slight oval and sew to Hat. With black yarn, embroider whiskers by making 1 long stitch for each whisker. Sew Eyes to Hat. Weave in ends. ♦

Mouth

Sheep

SUPPLIES

Worsted weight yarn in off-white (approx. 200 yards) and small amount of black

Size H/8 (5 mm) crochet hook or size needed to obtain gauge

Disappearing ink marking pen

Fiberfill stuffing

Stitch marker

Yarn needle

GAUGE

7 rnds of sc = 3" diameter circle

HAT

The Hat is crocheted with a combination of Single Crochet and Loop Stitch. Note: The loops will form on wrong side of work. You will turn the Hat loop-side out at the time of assembly.

With off-white yarn, make a magic ring, ch 1.

Rnd 1: 6 sc in ring, pull ring closed tight (6 sts).

Rnd 2: 2 lp st in each st around. Place marker for beginning of rnd and move marker up as each rnd is completed (12 sts).

Rnd 3: *lp st in next st, 2 lp st in next st* 6 times (18 sts).

Rnd 4: *lp st in next 2 sts, 2 lp st in next st* 6 times (24 sts).

Rnd 5: *lp st in next 3 sts, 2 lp st in next st* 6 times (30 sts).

Rnd 6: *lp st in next 4 sts, 2 lp st in next st* 6 times (36 sts).

Rnd 7: *lp st in next 5 sts, 2 lp st in next st* 6 times (42 sts).

Rnd 8: *lp st in next 6 sts, 2 lp st in next st* 6 times (48 sts).

Rnd 9: *lp st in next 7 sts, 2 lp st in next st* 6 times (54 sts).

• FOR SIZE SMALL:

Rnds 10-24: *sc in next 18 sts, lp st in next 36 sts* (54 sts).

Rnds 25-27: lp st in each st around. Fasten off.

• FOR SIZE MEDIUM:

Rnd 10: *lp st in next 8 sts, 2 lp st in next st* 6 times (60 sts).

Rnds 11-27: *sc in next 20 sts, lp st in next 40 sts* (60 sts).

Rnds 28-30: lp st in each st around. Fasten off.

• FOR SIZE LARGE:

Rnd 10: *lp st in next 8 sts, 2 lp st in next st* 6 times (60 sts).

Rnd 11: *lp st in next 9 sts, 2 lp st in next st* 6 times (66 sts).

Rnds 12-30: *sc in next 22 sts, lp st in next 44 sts* (66 sts).

Rnds 31-33: lp st in each st around. Fasten off.

EAR (MAKE 2)

With off-white yarn, make a magic ring, ch 1.

Rnd 1: 6 sc in ring, pull ring closed tight (6 sts).

Rnd 2: *sc in next 2 sts, 2 sc in next st* 2 times. Place marker for beginning of rnd and move marker up as each rnd is completed (8 sts).

Rnd 3: *sc in next 3 sts, 2 sc in next st" 2 times (10 sts).

Rnd 4: *sc in next 4 sts, 2 sc in next st" 2 times (12 sts).

Rnd 5: *sc in next 5 sts, 2 sc in next st" 2 times (14 sts).

Rnd 6: *sc in next 6 sts, 2 sc in next st" 2 times (16 sts).

Rnd 7: sc in each st around.

Rnd 8: *sc in next 6 sts, sc2tog* 2 times (14 sts).

Rnd 9: *sc in next 5 sts, sc2tog* 2 times (12 sts).

Rnd 10: *sc in next 4 sts, sc2tog* 2 times (10 sts).

Rnd 11: *sc in next 3 sts, sc2tog* 2 times (8 sts).

Sl st in next st. Fasten off with long tail.

EYE (MAKE 2)

With black yarn, make a magic ring, ch 1.

Rnd 1: 6 sc in ring, pull ring closed tight (6 sts).

Sl st in next st. Fasten off with long tail.

SNOUT

With off-white yarn, make a magic ring, ch 1.

Rnd 1: 6 sc in ring, pull ring closed tight (6 sts).

Rnd 2: 2 sc in each st around. Place marker for beginning of rnd and move marker up as each rnd is completed (12 sts).

Rnd 3: *sc in next st, 2 sc in next st* 6 times (18 sts).

Rnd 4: *sc in next 2 sts, 2 sc in next st* 6 times (24 sts).

Rnds 5-6: sc in each st around.

Sl st in next st. Fasten off with long tail.

ASSEMBLY

Turn hat loop-side out. With black yarn, embroider nose and mouth on Snout (see diagram). Use disappearing ink marking pen and circle template (see page 80) to draw position of Snout on face. Stuff Snout. Sew Snout, Eyes and Ears to Hat. Weave in ends. ♦

Nose & Mouth

Lion

SUPPLIES

Worsted weight yarn in golden-yellow (approx. 120 yards), and small amount of black plus super bulky Homespun yarn in variegated brown (approx. 15 yards)

Size H/8 (5 mm) crochet hook or size needed to obtain gauge

Polyester felt in walnut brown and black

Thread in walnut brown and black

Disappearing ink marking pen

Small piece of cardboard

Sewing Needle

Fiberfill stuffing

Stitch marker

Yarn needle

GAUGE

7 rnds of sc = 3" diameter circle

HAT

With golden-yellow yarn, make a magic ring, ch 1.

Rnd 1: 6 sc in ring, pull ring closed tight (6 sts).

Rnd 2: 2 sc in each st around. Place marker for beginning of rnd and move marker up as each rnd is completed (12 sts).

Rnd 3: *sc in next st, 2 sc in next st* 6 times (18 sts).

Rnd 4: *sc in next 2 sts, 2 sc in next st* 6 times (24 sts).

Rnd 5: *sc in next 3 sts, 2 sc in next st* 6 times (30 sts).

Rnd 6: *sc in next 4 sts, 2 sc in next st* 6 times (36 sts).

Rnd 7: *sc in next 5 sts, 2 sc in next st* 6 times (42 sts).

Rnd 8: *sc in next 6 sts, 2 sc in next st* 6 times (48 sts).

Rnd 9: *sc in next 7 sts, 2 sc in next st* 6 times (54 sts).

• FOR SIZE SMALL:

Rnds 10-27: sc in each st around. Fasten off.

• FOR SIZE MEDIUM:

Rnd 10: *sc in next 8 sts, 2 sc in next st* 6 times (60 sts).

Rnds 11-30: sc in each st around. Fasten off.

• FOR SIZE LARGE:

Rnd 10: *sc in next 8 sts, 2 sc in next st* 6 times (60 sts).

Rnd 11: *sc in next 9 sts, 2 sc in next st* 6 times (66 sts).

Rnds 12-33: sc in each st around. Fasten off.

EAR (MAKE 2)

With golden-yellow yarn, make a magic ring, ch 1.

Rnd 1: 6 sc in ring, pull ring closed tight (6 sts).

Rnd 2: 2 sc in each st around. Place marker for beginning of rnd and move marker up as each rnd is completed (12 sts).

Rnd 3: *sc in next st, 2 sc in next st* 6 times (18 sts).

Rnds 4-9: sc in each st around.

Fasten off with long tail.

SNOUT

With golden-yellow yarn, make a magic ring, ch 1.

Rnd 1: 6 sc in ring, pull ring closed tight (6 sts).

Rnd 2: 2 sc in each st around. Place marker for beginning of rnd and move marker up as each rnd is completed (12 sts).

Rnd 3: *sc in next st, 2 sc in next st* 6 times (18 sts).

Rnd 4: *sc in next 2 sts, 2 sc in next st* 6 times (24 sts).

Rnd 5: *sc in next 3 sts, 2 sc in next st* 6 times (30 sts).

Rnds 6-7: sc in each st around.

Sl st in next st. Fasten off with long tail.

MANE

You will need many 4-inch pieces of variegated brown Homespun yarn to make the Mane. To quickly cut the strands, wrap yarn widthwise around a 2" x 6" piece of cardboard. On one side, insert scissors between cardboard and yarn—and cut. Flatten Hat with fingers. Put hook through a st on crease (see Figure A) and follow instructions for Fringe (see page 13) using 1 strand of yarn. Repeat fringe in each st around crease. Fill in center front hairline with 6 more strands of fringe in front of 1st row (see arrow, Figure B). Work a 2nd row of fringe behind 1st row (see arrow, Figure C). Trim straggly ends.

EYE (MAKE 2)

Cut a 3/4" circle of walnut brown felt and a 1/2" circle of black felt (see templates, page 80). Stack black circle on brown circle and whip stitch in place.

NOSE

With black yarn, make a magic ring, ch 1.

Rnd 1: 5 sc in ring, pull ring closed tight (5 sts).

Sl st in next st. Fasten off with long tail.

FIGURE A

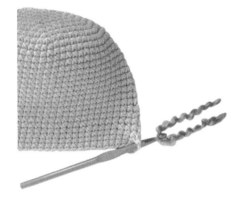

FIGURE B

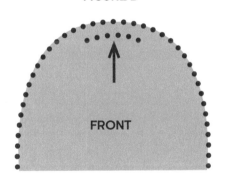

FRONT

FIGURE C

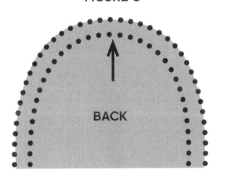

BACK

ASSEMBLY

Sew Nose to Snout just below center and embroider straight stitch mouth (see diagram). Use template (see page 78) and disappearing ink marking pen to draw position of Snout on Hat. Stuff Snout, pull gently at top and bottom to make a slightly oval shape and sew to Hat. Sew Eyes to Hat. Sew Ears to Hat between rows of fringe. Weave in ends. ♦

Mouth

Frog

SUPPLIES

Worsted weight yarn in green (approx. 120 yards) plus small amount of white, raspberry and pink

Size H/8 (5 mm) crochet hook or size needed to obtain gauge

Disappearing ink marking pen

Polyester felt in black

Fiberfill stuffing

Black thread

Sewing needle

Hole punch

Stitch marker

Yarn needle

GAUGE

7 rnds of sc = 3" diameter circle

HAT

Wtih green yarn, make a magic ring, ch 1.

Rnd 1: 6 sc in ring, pull ring closed tight (6 sts).

Rnd 2: 2 sc in each st around. Place marker for beginning of rnd and move marker up as each rnd is completed (12 sts).

Rnd 3: *sc in next st, 2 sc in next st* 6 times (18 sts).

Rnd 4: *sc in next 2 sts, 2 sc in next st* 6 times (24 sts).

Rnd 5: *sc in next 3 sts, 2 sc in next st* 6 times (30 sts).

Rnd 6: *sc in next 4 sts, 2 sc in next st* 6 times (36 sts).

Rnd 7: *sc in next 5 sts, 2 sc in next st* 6 times (42 sts).

Rnd 8: *sc in next 6 sts, 2 sc in next st* 6 times (48 sts).

Rnd 9: *sc in next 7 sts, 2 sc in next st* 6 times (54 sts).

• FOR SIZE SMALL:

Rnds 10-27: sc in each st around. Fasten off.

• FOR SIZE MEDIUM:

Rnd 10: *sc in next 8 sts, 2 sc in next st* 6 times (60 sts).

Rnds 11-30: sc in each st around. Fasten off.

• FOR SIZE LARGE:

Rnd 10: *sc in next 8 sts, 2 sc in next st* 6 times (60 sts).

Rnd 11: *sc in next 9 sts, 2 sc in next st* 6 times (66 sts).

Rnds 12-33: sc in each st around. Fasten off.

INNER EYE (MAKE 2)

Cut a 1/2" circle of black felt (see template, page 80).

EYE RIM (MAKE 2)

With white yarn, make a magic ring, ch 1.

Rnd 1: 4 sc in ring, pull ring closed tight (4 sts).

Rnd 2: 2 sc in each st around (8 sts).

Sl st in next st. Fasten off with long tail.

OUTER EYE (MAKE 2)

With green yarn, make a magic ring, ch 1.

Rnd 1: 6 sc in ring, pull ring closed tight (6 sts).

Rnd 2: 2 sc in each st around. Place marker for beginning of rnd and move marker up as each rnd is completed (12 sts).

Rnd 3: *sc in next st, 2 sc in next st* 6 times (18 sts).

Rnd 4: *sc in next 2 sts, 2 sc in next st* 6 times (24 sts).

Rnds 5-9: sc in each st around.

Fasten off with long tail.

BOW (OPTIONAL)

With pink yarn, ch 6 loosely.

Row 1: sc in 2nd chain from hook and in each remaining ch across (5 sts).

Rows 2-3: ch 1, turn, sc in each st across (5 sts).

Rnd 4: sc in each st around next 3 sides. Join with sl st to next st. Fasten off.

Weave ends into wrong side. With a scrap of yarn, tie tightly across center of rectangle. Wrap 1 end around center several times to make a pretty pinched middle. Knot ends together leaving long tails.

MOUTH

To mark mouth, trace template onto office paper (see page 79). Punch holes in tips. Place template in position and dot with disappearing ink into the holes. Remove paper and connect dots.

With raspberry yarn, sew along outline with running stitch. Now sew in opposite direction to fill in the spaces, inserting needle through a bit of the stitches on either side to avoid gaps.

ASSEMBLY

Sew Inner Eyes to Eye Rims. Sew Eye Rims to front of Outer Eyes. Sew Bow to top of one Eye, if desired. Stuff Eyes with fiberfill. Mark position of Eyes on Hat with disappearing ink marking pen and circle templates (see page 80). Sew Eyes to Hat. Weave in ends. ♦

Panda

SUPPLIES

Worsted weight yarn in white (approx. 110 yards) and black (approx. 35 yards) plus small amount of pink

Size H/8 (5 mm) crochet hook or size needed to obtain gauge

Disappearing ink marking pen

Cardboard scrap

Fiberfill stuffing

Stitch marker

Yarn needle

GAUGE

7 rnds of sc = 3" diameter circle

HAT

With white yarn, make a magic ring, ch 1.

Rnd 1: 6 sc in ring, pull ring closed tight (6 sts).

Rnd 2: 2 sc in each st around. Place marker for beginning of rnd and move marker up as each rnd is completed (12 sts).

Rnd 3: *sc in next st, 2 sc in next st* 6 times (18 sts).

Rnd 4: *sc in next 2 sts, 2 sc in next st* 6 times (24 sts).

Rnd 5: *sc in next 3 sts, 2 sc in next st* 6 times (30 sts).

Rnd 6: *sc in next 4 sts, 2 sc in next st* 6 times (36 sts).

Rnd 7: *sc in next 5 sts, 2 sc in next st* 6 times (42 sts).

Rnd 8: *sc in next 6 sts, 2 sc in next st* 6 times (48 sts).

Rnd 9: *sc in next 7 sts, 2 sc in next st* 6 times (54 sts).

• FOR SIZE SMALL:

Rnds 10-27: sc in each st around. Fasten off.

• FOR SIZE MEDIUM:

Rnd 10: *sc in next 8 sts, 2 sc in next st* 6 times (60 sts).

Rnds 11-30: sc in each st around. Fasten off.

• FOR SIZE LARGE:

Rnd 10: *sc in next 8 sts, 2 sc in next st* 6 times (60 sts).

Rnd 11: *sc in next 9 sts, 2 sc in next st* 6 times (66 sts).

Rnds 12-33: sc in each st around. Fasten off.

EYE RIM (MAKE 2)

The Eye Rim is made in 2 sections.

Part A

With black yarn, make a magic ring, ch 1.

Rnd 1: 6 sc in ring, pull ring closed tight (6 sts).

Rnd 2: 2 sc in each st around. Place marker for beginning of rnd and move marker up as each rnd is completed (12 sts).

Rnd 3: *sc in next st, 2 sc in next st* 6 times (18 sts).

Rnd 4: *2 sc in next st, sc in next 2 sts* 6 times (24 sts).

Sl st in next st. Fasten off with long tail.

Part B

With black yarn, ch 2.

Row 1: 3 sc in 2nd ch from hook (3 sts).

Row 2: ch 1, turn, 2 sc in each st across (6 sts).

Row 3: ch 1, turn, *sc in next st, 2 sc in next st* 3 times (9 sts).

Row 4: ch 1, turn, *sc in next 2 sts, 2 sc in next st* 3 times (12 sts).

Fasten off with long tail. Place straight side of Part B anywhere against side of Part A and sew together.

OUTER EYE (MAKE 2)

With white yarn, make a magic ring, ch 1.

Rnd 1: 6 sc in ring, pull ring closed tight (6 sts).

Rnd 2: 2 sc in each st around (12 sts).

Sl st in next st. Fasten off with long tail.

INNER EYE (MAKE 2)

With black yarn, make a magic ring, ch 1.

Rnd 1: 6 sc in ring, pull ring closed tight (6 sts).

Sl st in next st. Fasten off with long tail.

EAR (MAKE 2)

Cut a rectangle of cardboard measuring 2" x 6". Wrap black yarn widthwise around the cardboard 75 times. Carefully slide yarn off cardboard. Using a scrap of yarn, tie bundle together tightly around the middle. Wrap tails of tie to opposite side and tie again. Cut loops open. (See Pom Poms, page 15.) Fluff pom pom and trim ends into a nice round shape.

SNOUT

With white yarn, make a magic ring, ch 1.

Rnd 1: 6 sc in ring, pull ring closed tight (6 sts).

Rnd 2: 2 sc in each st around. Place marker for beginning of rnd and move marker up as each rnd is completed (12 sts).

Rnd 3: sc in each st around.

Rnd 4: *sc in next st, 2 sc in next st* 6 times (18 sts).

Rnd 5: sc in each st around.

Rnd 6: *sc in next 2 sts, 2 sc in next st* 6 times (24 sts).

Rnd 7: sc in each st around.

Sl st in next st. Fasten off with long tail.

NOSE

With black yarn, make a magic ring, ch 1.

Rnd 1: 5 sc in ring, pull ring closed tight (5 sts).

Sl st in next st. Fasten off with long tail.

ASSEMBLY

Sew Nose to Snout. With pink yarn, embroider mouth (see diagram below). Mark position of Snout on Hat with disappearing ink marking pen and circle template (see page 80). Stuff Snout and sew to Hat. Tie Ears to Hat. Sew Inner Eyes to Outer Eyes. Sew Outer Eyes to Eye Rims. Sew Eye Rims to Hat. Weave in ends. ♦

Mouth

Stegosaurus

SUPPLIES

Worsted weight yarn in blue (approx. 120 yards) and gold (approx. 85 yards) plus small amount of white and black

Size H/8 (5 mm) crochet hook or size needed to obtain gauge

Polyester felt in golden-yellow and black

Thread in golden-yellow and black

Disappearing ink marking pen

Sewing needle

Fiberfill stuffing

Stitch marker

Yarn needle

GAUGE

7 rnds of sc = 3" diameter circle

HAT

With blue yarn, make a magic ring, ch 1.

Rnd 1: 6 sc in ring, pull ring closed tight (6 sts).

Rnd 2: 2 sc in each st around. Place marker for beginning of rnd and move marker up as each rnd is completed (12 sts).

Rnd 3: *sc in next st, 2 sc in next st* 6 times (18 sts).

Rnd 4: *sc in next 2 sts, 2 sc in next st* 6 times (24 sts).

Rnd 5: *sc in next 3 sts, 2 sc in next st* 6 times (30 sts).

Rnd 6: *sc in next 4 sts, 2 sc in next st* 6 times (36 sts).

Rnd 7: *sc in next 5 sts, 2 sc in next st* 6 times (42 sts).

Rnd 8: *sc in next 6 sts, 2 sc in next st* 6 times (48 sts).

Rnd 9: *sc in next 7 sts, 2 sc in next st* 6 times (54 sts).

• FOR SIZE SMALL:

Rnds 10-27: sc in each st around. Fasten off.

• FOR SIZE MEDIUM:

Rnd 10: *sc in next 8 sts, 2 sc in next st* 6 times (60 sts).

Rnds 11-30: sc in each st around. Fasten off.

• FOR SIZE LARGE:

Rnd 10: *sc in next 8 sts, 2 sc in next st* 6 times (60 sts).

Rnd 11: *sc in next 9 sts, 2 sc in next st* 6 times (66 sts).

Rnds 12-33: sc in each st around. Fasten off.

HEAD

With blue yarn, make a magic ring, ch 1.

Rnd 1: 6 sc in ring, pull ring closed tight (6 sts).

Rnd 2: 2 sc in each st around. Place marker for beginning of rnd and move marker up as each rnd is completed (12 sts).

Rnd 3: *sc in next st, 2 sc in next st* 6 times (18 sts).

Rnds 4-5: sc in each st around.

Rnd 6: *sc in next 2 sts, 2 sc in next st* 6 times (24 sts).

Rnds 7-8: sc in each st around.

Rnd 9: *sc in next 3 sts, 2 sc in next st* 6 times (30 sts).

Rnds 10-11: sc in each st around.

Rnd 12: *sc in next 4 sts, 2 sc in next st* 6 times (36 sts).

Rnds 13-14: sc in each st around.

Rnd 15: *sc in next 5 sts, 2 sc in next st* 6 times (42 sts).

Rnds 16-17: sc in each st around.

Fasten off with long tail.

SMALL PLATE (MAKE 4)

With gold yarn, make a magic ring, ch 1.

Rnd 1: 6 sc in ring, pull ring closed tight (6 sts).

Rnd 2: *sc in next 2 sts, 2 sc in next st* 2 times. Place marker for beginning of rnd and move marker up as each rnd is completed (8 sts).

Rnd 3: sc in each st around.

Rnd 4: *sc in next 2 sts, sc2tog* 2 times (6 sts).

Sl st in next st. Fasten off with long tail. Pinch tip into a nice point.

MEDIUM PLATE (MAKE 4)

With gold yarn, make a magic ring, ch 1.

Rnd 1: 6 sc in ring, pull ring closed tight (6 sts).

Rnd 2: *sc in next 2 sts, 2 sc in next st* 2 times. Place marker for beginning of rnd and move marker up as each rnd is completed (8 sts).

Rnd 3: *sc in next 3 sts, 2 sc in next st* 2 times (10 sts).

Rnd 4: *sc in next 4 sts, 2 sc in next st* 2 times (12 sts).

Rnd 5: sc in each st around.

Rnd 6: *sc in next 4 sts, sc2tog* 2 times (10 sts).

Rnd 7: *sc in next 3 sts, sc2tog* 2 times (8 sts).

Sl st in next st. Fasten off with long tail. Pinch tip into a nice point.

LARGE PLATE (MAKE 6)

With gold yarn, make a magic ring, ch 1.

Rnd 1: 6 sc in ring, pull ring closed tight (6 sts).

Rnd 2: *sc in next 2 sts, 2 sc in next st* 2 times. Place marker for beginning of rnd and move marker up as each rnd is completed (8 sts).

Rnd 3: *sc in next 3 sts, 2 sc in next st* 2 times (10 sts).

Rnd 4: *sc in next 4 sts, 2 sc in next st* 2 times (12 sts).

Rnd 5: *sc in next 5 sts, 2 sc in next st* 2 times (14 sts).

Rnd 6: *sc in next 6 sts, 2 sc in next st* 2 times (16 sts).

Rnd 7: *sc in next 7 sts, 2 sc in next st* 2 times (18 sts).

Rnd 8: sc in each st around.

Rnd 9: *sc in next 7 sts, sc2tog* 2 times (16 sts).

Rnd 10: *sc in next 6 sts, sc2tog* 2 times (14 sts).

Rnd 11: *sc in next 5 sts, sc2tog* 2 times (12 sts).

Rnd 12: *sc in next 4 sts, sc2tog* 2 times (10 sts).

Sl st in next st. Fasten off with long tail. Pinch tip into a nice point.

OUTER EYE (MAKE 2)

With white yarn, make a magic ring, ch 1.

Rnd 1: 6 sc in ring, pull ring closed tight (6 sts).

Rnd 2: 2 sc in each st around. Place marker for beginning of rnd and move marker up as each rnd is completed (12 sts).

Rnds 3-4: sc in each st around.

Fasten off with long tail.

INNER EYE (MAKE 2)

Cut a 5/8" circle of golden-yellow felt and a 3/8" circle of black felt (see templates, page 80). Stack black circle on golden-yellow circle and whip stitch in place.

EYELID (MAKE 2)

With blue yarn, ch 2.

Row 1: 3 sc in 2nd ch from hook.

Row 2: ch 1, turn, 2 sc in next 3 sts (6 sts).

Row 3: ch 1, turn, *sc in next st, 2 sc in next st* 3 times (9 sts).

Row 4: ch 1, turn, *sc in next 2 sts, 2 sc in next st* 3 times (12 sts).

Fasten off with long tail. Weave in short tail from starting point.

ASSEMBLY

Lay Hat down flat and draw a line with disappearing ink marking pen along the center (see Figure A). Flip Hat over and repeat on other side. Sew Inner Eyes to center of Outer Eyes with whip stitch. Stuff Eyes lightly and sew to Head. Place Eyelids so that straight side slants across Eyes and sew in position. With a double strand of black yarn, embroider 2 French knots on Head for nostrils. Flatten Head (do not stuff) and sew the open end closed. Sew Head to Hat so that Head extends below lower edge of Hat (see Figure B). Behind Head, sew Plates to Hat in 2 rows (1 row on each side of center line) with Plates for each row in this order: 1 Small Plate, 1 Medium Plate, 3 Large Plates, 1 Medium Plate and 1 Small Plate. Tip: To sew on Plates, I find it easiest to lay Plates on their side and whip stitch securely to Hat (see Figure B). Then raise Plates up into position. To hide yarn tails from plates, thread tail onto yarn needle, push needle up through center of plate and out at the tip. Trim yarn flush with tip of plate and tug on plate to conceal any evidence of yarn tail. Weave in remaining ends. ♦

FIGURE A

FIGURE B

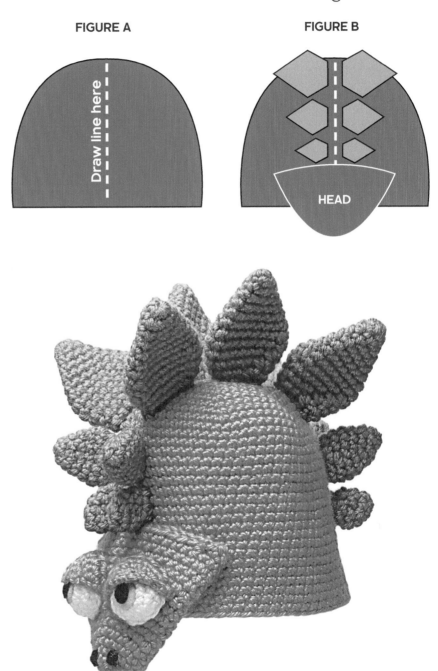

Draw line here

HEAD

Duck

SUPPLIES

Worsted weight yarn in yellow (approx. 100 yards) plus small amount of orange and white

Size H/8 (5 mm) crochet hook or size needed to obtain gauge

Polyester felt in black

Black thread

Sewing needle

Stitch marker

Yarn needle

GAUGE

7 rnds of sc = 3" diameter circle

HAT

With yellow yarn, make a magic ring, ch 1.

Rnd 1: 6 sc in ring, pull ring closed tight (6 sts).

Rnd 2: 2 sc in each st around. Place marker for beginning of rnd and move marker up as each rnd is completed (12 sts).

Rnd 3: *sc in next st, 2 sc in next st* 6 times (18 sts).

Rnd 4: *sc in next 2 sts, 2 sc in next st* 6 times (24 sts).

Rnd 5: *sc in next 3 sts, 2 sc in next st* 6 times (30 sts).

Rnd 6: *sc in next 4 sts, 2 sc in next st* 6 times (36 sts).

Rnd 7: *sc in next 5 sts, 2 sc in next st* 6 times (42 sts).

Rnd 8: *sc in next 6 sts, 2 sc in next st* 6 times (48 sts).

Rnd 9: *sc in next 7 sts, 2 sc in next st* 6 times (54 sts).

• FOR SIZE SMALL:

Rnds 10-27: sc in each st around. Fasten off.

• FOR SIZE MEDIUM:

Rnd 10: *sc in next 8 sts, 2 sc in next st* 6 times (60 sts).

Rnds 11-30: sc in each st around. Fasten off.

• FOR SIZE LARGE:

Rnd 10: *sc in next 8 sts, 2 sc in next st* 6 times (60 sts).

Rnd 11: *sc in next 9 sts, 2 sc in next st* 6 times (66 sts).

Rnds 12-33: sc in each st around. Fasten off.

OUTER EYE (MAKE 2)

The eye is worked around a foundation chain.

With white yarn, ch 4 loosely.

Rnd 1: starting in 2nd ch from hook, *sc in next 2 sts, 3 sc in next st* 2 times (10 sts).

St st in next st. Fasten off with long tail.

INNER EYE (MAKE 2)

Cut a 1/2" circle of black felt (see template, page 80).

BEAK

With orange yarn, make a magic ring, ch 1.

Rnd 1: 6 sc in ring, pull ring closed tight (6 sts).

Rnd 2: 2 sc in each st around. Place marker for beginning of rnd and move marker up as each rnd is completed (12 sts).

Rnd 3: *sc in next st, 2 sc in next st* 6 times (18 sts).

Rnd 4: *sc in next 2 sts, 2 sc in next st* 6 times (24 sts).

Rnd 5: *sc in next 3 sts, 2 sc in next st* 6 times (30 sts).

Rnd 6: *sc in next 4 sts, 2 sc in next st* 6 times (36 sts).

Fasten off with long tail.

TUFT

Cut four 6-inch strands of yellow yarn. Lay strands together side by side and attach to top of Hat using Fringe technique (see page 13). Trim ends even.

ASSEMBLY

Fold Beak in half, wrong sides together. Make 2 whip stitches at each corner to hold the crease. Sew Inner Eyes off-center to Outer Eyes. Sew Eyes and Beak to Hat. Weave in ends. ♦

SUPPLIES

Worsted weight yarn in tan fleck (approx. 105 yards) plus small amount of brown fleck, black and pink

Size H/8 (5 mm) crochet hook or size needed to obtain gauge

Fiberfill stuffing

Cardboard scrap

Stitch marker

Yarn needle

GAUGE

7 rnds of sc = 3" diameter circle

HAT

With tan fleck yarn, make a magic ring, ch 1.

Rnd 1: 6 sc in ring, pull ring closed tight (6 sts).

Rnd 2: 2 sc in each st around. Place marker for beginning of rnd and move marker up as each rnd is completed (12 sts).

Rnd 3: *sc in next st, 2 sc in next st* 6 times (18 sts).

Rnd 4: *sc in next 2 sts, 2 sc in next st* 6 times (24 sts).

Rnd 5: *sc in next 3 sts, 2 sc in next st* 6 times (30 sts).

Rnd 6: *sc in next 4 sts, 2 sc in next st* 6 times (36 sts).

Rnd 7: *sc in next 5 sts, 2 sc in next st* 6 times (42 sts).

Rnd 8: *sc in next 6 sts, 2 sc in next st* 6 times (48 sts).

Rnd 9: *sc in next 7 sts, 2 sc in next st* 6 times (54 sts).

• FOR SIZE SMALL:

Rnds 10-27: sc in each st around. Fasten off.

• FOR SIZE MEDIUM:

Rnd 10: *sc in next 8 sts, 2 sc in next st* 6 times (60 sts).

Rnds 11-30: sc in each st around. Fasten off.

• FOR SIZE LARGE:

Rnd 10: *sc in next 8 sts, 2 sc in next st* 6 times (60 sts).

Rnd 11: *sc in next 9 sts, 2 sc in next st* 6 times (66 sts).

Rnds 12-33: sc in each st around. Fasten off.

EYE (MAKE 2)

With black yarn, make a magic ring, ch 1.

Rnd 1: 10 sc in ring, pull ring closed tight (10 sts).

Sl st in next st. Fasten off with long tail.

NOSE

With black yarn, make a magic ring, ch 1.

Rnd 1: 6 sc in ring, pull ring closed tight (6 sts).

Rnd 2: 2 sc in each st around. Place marker for beginning of rnd and move marker up as each rnd is completed (12 sts).

Rnd 3: sc in each st around.

Rnd 4: sc2tog 6 times (6 sts).

Fasten off with long tail. Pack in stuffing with eraser end of pencil. Sew opening shut.

TONGUE (OPTIONAL)

With pink yarn, ch 2.

Row 1: 3 sc in 2nd ch from hook (3 sts).

Row 2: ch 1, turn, 2 sc in each st across (6 sts).

Row 3: ch 1, turn, *sc in next st, 2 sc in next st* 3 times (9 sts).

Fasten off with long tail. Tie the two tail ends together tightly.

SNOUT

Cut a square of cardboard measuring 4" x 4". Wrap tan fleck yarn around cardboard 25 times. Carefully slide yarn off cardboard. Using a scrap of matching yarn, tie bundle together tightly around the middle. Wrap tails to opposite side and tie again. Cut loops open. Flatten pom pom so that all strands radiate from the center (see Figure A) and set aside.

EAR (MAKE 2)

Cut a rectangle of cardboard measuring 4" x 14". Wrap brown fleck yarn lengthwise around cardboard 12 times. Carefully slide yarn off cardboard. Using a scrap of matching yarn, tie bundle together tightly around the middle. Cut loops open. *Note: A cookie sheet can be substituted for cardboard to wrap the ears.*

ASSEMBLY

To attach Snout to Hat, thread yarn needle with long tail of Nose. Insert needle through center of Snout (see Figure A) and then through Hat. Push needle up through Nose and back down through Hat several times to secure. At base of Nose, tuck Tongue under top layer of Snout yarns and sew in place. Sew Eyes to Hat. For eyebrows, embroider straight stitches over each eye (see Eyebrow Guide). Tie Ears to top of Hat. Trim stray strands on Snout. Trim Ears to desired length. Weave in ends. ♦

FIGURE A

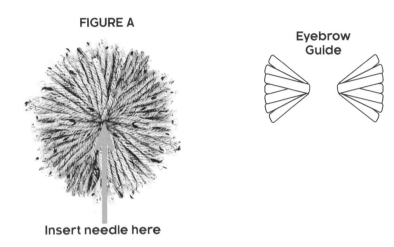

Insert needle here

Eyebrow Guide

Pig

SUPPLIES

Worsted weight yarn in pink (approx. 110 yards) and small amount of black

Size H/8 (5 mm) crochet hook or size needed to obtain gauge

Disappearing ink marking pen

Fiberfill stuffing

Stitch marker

Yarn needle

GAUGE

7 rnds of sc = 3" diameter circle

HAT

With pink yarn, make a magic ring, ch 1.

Rnd 1: 6 sc in ring, pull ring closed tight (6 sts).

Rnd 2: 2 sc in each st around. Place marker for beginning of rnd and move marker up as each rnd is completed (12 sts).

Rnd 3: *sc in next st, 2 sc in next st* 6 times (18 sts).

Rnd 4: *sc in next 2 sts, 2 sc in next st* 6 times (24 sts).

Rnd 5: *sc in next 3 sts, 2 sc in next st* 6 times (30 sts).

Rnd 6: *sc in next 4 sts, 2 sc in next st* 6 times (36 sts).

Rnd 7: *sc in next 5 sts, 2 sc in next st* 6 times (42 sts).

Rnd 8: *sc in next 6 sts, 2 sc in next st* 6 times (48 sts).

Rnd 9: *sc in next 7 sts, 2 sc in next st* 6 times (54 sts).

• FOR SIZE SMALL:

Rnds 10-27: sc in each st around. Fasten off.

• FOR SIZE MEDIUM:

Rnd 10: *sc in next 8 sts, 2 sc in next st* 6 times (60 sts).

Rnds 11-30: sc in each st around. Fasten off.

• FOR SIZE LARGE:

Rnd 10: *sc in next 8 sts, 2 sc in next st* 6 times (60 sts).

Rnd 11: *sc in next 9 sts, 2 sc in next st* 6 times (66 sts).

Rnds 12-33: sc in each st around. Fasten off.

EYE (MAKE 2)

With black yarn, make a magic ring, ch 1.

Rnd 1: 6 sc in ring, pull ring closed tight (6 sts).

Sl st in next st. Fasten off with long tail.

EAR (MAKE 2)

With pink yarn, make a magic ring, ch 1.

Rnd 1: 6 sc in ring, pull ring closed tight (6 sts).

Rnd 2: *sc in next 2 sts, 2 sc in next st* 2 times. Place marker for beginning of rnd and move marker up as each rnd is completed (8 sts).

Rnd 3: *sc in next 3 sts, 2 sc in next st* 2 times (10 sts).

Rnd 4: *sc in next 4 sts, 2 sc in next st* 2 times (12 sts).

Rnd 5: *sc in next 5 sts, 2 sc in next st* 2 times (14 sts).

Rnd 6: *sc in next 6 sts, 2 sc in next st* 2 times (16 sts).

Rnd 7: *sc in next 7 sts, 2 sc in next st* 2 times (18 sts).

Rnd 8: *sc in next 8 sts, 2 sc in next st* 2 times (20 sts).

Rnds 9-10: sc in each st around.

Sl st in next st. Fasten off with long tail.

SNOUT

With pink yarn, make a magic ring, ch 1.

Rnd 1: 6 sc in ring, pull ring closed tight (6 sts).

Rnd 2: 2 sc in each st around. Place marker for beginning of rnd and move marker up as each rnd is completed (12 sts).

Rnd 3: *sc in next st, 2 sc in next st* 6 times (18 sts).

Rnd 4: *sc in next 2 sts, 2 sc in next st* 6 times (24 sts).

Rnds 5-8: sc in each st around.

Sl st in next st. Fasten off with long tail. With a double strand of black yarn, embroider 2 French knots for nostrils.

TAIL

With pink yarn, ch 21 loosely.

Row 1: 3 sc in 2nd ch from hook and in each ch across (60 sts).

Fasten off with long tail.

ASSEMBLY

Mark position of Snout with disappearing ink marking pen and circle template (see page 80). Stuff Snout and sew to Hat. Sew Ears and Eyes in place. Sew Tail to center back of Hat. Weave in ends. ♦

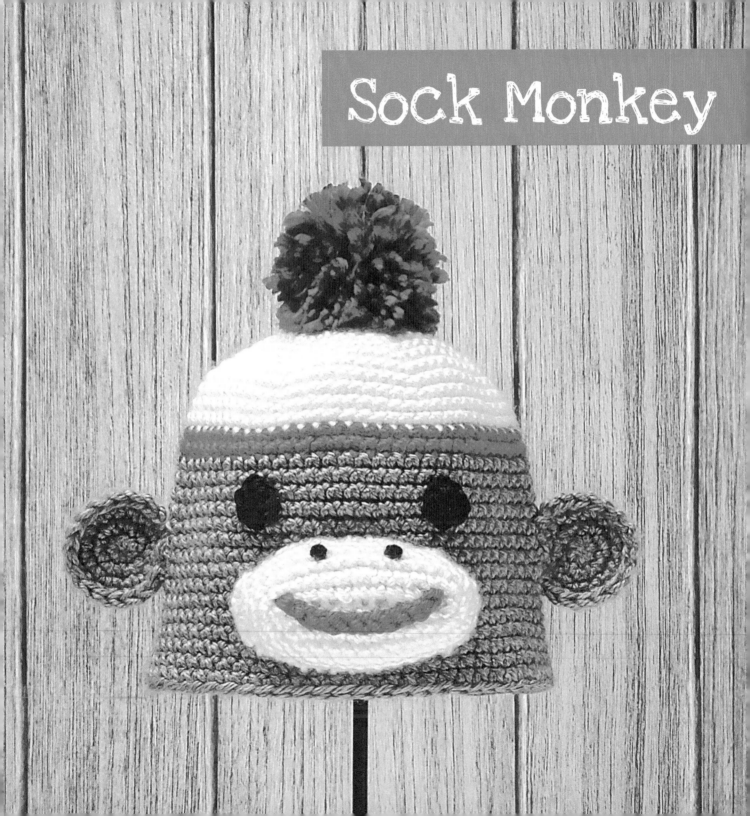

Sock Monkey

SUPPLIES

Worsted weight yarn in gray heather (approx. 50 yards) and off-white (approx. 45 yards) plus small amount of dark red and black

Size H/8 (5 mm) crochet hook or size needed to obtain gauge

Disappearing ink marking pen

Small piece of cardboard

Fiberfill stuffing

Stitch marker

Yarn needle

GAUGE

7 rnds of sc = 3" diameter circle

HAT

With off-white yarn, make a magic ring, ch 1.

Rnd 1: 6 sc in ring, pull ring closed tight (6 sts).

Rnd 2: 2 sc in each st around. Place marker for beginning of rnd and move marker up as each rnd is completed (12 sts).

Rnd 3: *sc in next st, 2 sc in next st* 6 times (18 sts).

Rnd 4: *sc in next 2 sts, 2 sc in next st* 6 times (24 sts).

Rnd 5: *sc in next 3 sts, 2 sc in next st* 6 times (30 sts).

Rnd 6: *sc in next 4 sts, 2 sc in next st* 6 times (36 sts).

Rnd 7: *sc in next 5 sts, 2 sc in next st* 6 times (42 sts).

Rnd 8: *sc in next 6 sts, 2 sc in next st* 6 times (48 sts).

Rnd 9: *sc in next 7 sts, 2 sc in next st* 6 times (54 sts).

• FOR SIZE SMALL:

Rnds 10-11: sc in each st around; change to red yarn in last st.

Rnds 12-13: sc in each st around; change to gray yarn in last st.

Rnds 14-27: sc in each st around. Fasten off.

• FOR SIZE MEDIUM:

Rnd 10: *sc in next 8 sts, 2 sc in next st* 6 times (60 sts).

Rnds 11-13: sc in each st around; change to red yarn in last st.

Rnds 14-15: sc in each st around; change to gray yarn in last st.

Rnds 16-30: sc in each st around. Fasten off.

• FOR SIZE LARGE:

Rnd 10: *sc in next 8 sts, 2 sc in next st* 6 times (60 sts).

Rnd 11: *sc in next 9 sts, 2 sc in next st* 6 times (66 sts).

Rnds 12-15: sc in each st around; change to red yarn in last st.

Rnds 16-17: sc in each st around; change to gray yarn in last st.

Rnds 18-33: sc in each st around. Fasten off.

SNOUT

The Snout is worked around a foundation chain.

With off-white yarn, ch 11 loosely.

Rnd 1: starting in 2nd ch from hook *sc in next 9 sts, 3 sc in next st* 2 times. Place marker for beginning of rnd and move marker up as each rnd is completed (24 sts).

Rnd 2: *sc in next 4 sts, 2 sc in next st, sc in next 4 sts, 2 sc in next 3 sts* 2 times (32 sts).

Rnds 3-5: sc in each st around.

Sl st in next st. Fasten off with long tail.

EYE (MAKE 2)

With black yarn, make a magic ring, ch 1.

Rnd 1: 6 sc in ring, pull ring closed tight (6 sts).

Sl st in next st. Fasten off with long tail.

MOUTH

With red yarn, ch st until your work measures 3" long. Fasten off with long tail.

EAR (MAKE 2)

With gray yarn, make a magic ring, ch 1.

Rnd 1: 6 sc in ring, pull ring closed tight (6 sts).

Rnd 2: 2 sc in each st around. Place marker for beginning of rnd and move marker up as each rnd is completed (12 sts).

Rnd 3: *sc in next st, 2 sc in next st* 6 times (18 sts).

Rnd 4: sc in each st around.

Sl st in next st. Fasten off with long tail.

POM POM

Cut a rectangle of cardboard measuring 2" x 6". Wrap red yarn widthwise around cardboard 75 times. Carefully slide yarn off cardboard. Using a scrap of yarn, tie bundle together tightly around the middle. Wrap tails of tie to opposite side and tie again. Cut loops open. (See Pom Poms, page 15.) Fluff pom pom and trim ends into a nice round shape.

ASSEMBLY

Sew Mouth in a curve to center of Snout. With black yarn, embroider 2 French knots on top of Snout. Use template (see page 78) and disappearing ink marking pen to draw position of Snout on Hat. Stuff Snout and sew to Hat. Sew Eyes and Ears to Hat. Tie Pom Pom on top. Weave in ends. ♦

Cow

SUPPLIES

Worsted weight yarn in white (approx. 100 yards) and black (approx. 50 yards) plus small amount of brown, light pink and dark pink

Size H/8 (5 mm) crochet hook or size needed to obtain gauge

Polyester felt in walnut brown and black

Thread in walnut brown and black

Disappearing ink marking pen

Sewing needle

Fiberfill stuffing

Stitch marker

Yarn needle

GAUGE

7 rnds of sc = 3" diameter circle

HAT

With white yarn, make a magic ring, ch 1.

Rnd 1: 6 sc in ring, pull ring closed tight (6 sts).

Rnd 2: 2 sc in each st around. Place marker for beginning of rnd and move marker up as each rnd is completed (12 sts).

Rnd 3: *sc in next st, 2 sc in next st* 6 times (18 sts).

Rnd 4: *sc in next 2 sts, 2 sc in next st* 6 times (24 sts).

Rnd 5: *sc in next 3 sts, 2 sc in next st* 6 times (30 sts).

Rnd 6: *sc in next 4 sts, 2 sc in next st* 6 times (36 sts).

Rnd 7: *sc in next 5 sts, 2 sc in next st* 6 times (42 sts).

Rnd 8: *sc in next 6 sts, 2 sc in next st* 6 times (48 sts).

Rnd 9: *sc in next 7 sts, 2 sc in next st* 6 times (54 sts).

• FOR SIZE SMALL:

Rnds 10-27: sc in each st around. Fasten off.

• FOR SIZE MEDIUM:

Rnd 10: *sc in next 8 sts, 2 sc in next st* 6 times (60 sts).

Rnds 11-30: sc in each st around. Fasten off.

• FOR SIZE LARGE:

Rnd 10: *sc in next 8 sts, 2 sc in next st* 6 times (60 sts).

Rnd 11: *sc in next 9 sts, 2 sc in next st* 6 times (66 sts).

Rnds 12-33: sc in each st around. Fasten off.

EYE (MAKE 2)

Cut a 3/4" circle of walnut brown felt and a 1/2" circle of black felt (see templates, page 80). Stack black circle on brown circle and whip stitch in place.

SNOUT

The Snout is worked around a foundation chain.

With pink yarn, ch 8 loosely.

Rnd 1: starting in 2nd ch from hook *sc in next 6 sts, 3 sc in next st* 2 times. Place marker for beginning of rnd and move marker up as each rnd is completed (18 sts).

Rnd 2: *sc in next 6 sts, 2 sc in next 3 sts* 2 times (24 sts).

Rnds 3-5: sc in each st around.

Sl st in next st. Fasten off with long tail.

EAR (MAKE 2)

With black yarn, make a magic ring, ch 1.

Rnd 1: 6 sc in ring, pull ring closed tight (6 sts).

Rnd 2: *sc in next 2 sts, 2 sc in next st* 2 times. Place marker for beginning of rnd and move marker up as each rnd is completed (8 sts).

Rnd 3: *sc in next 3 sts, 2 sc in next st" 2 times (10 sts).

Rnd 4: *sc in next 4 sts, 2 sc in next st" 2 times (12 sts).

Rnd 5: *sc in next 5 sts, 2 sc in next st" 2 times (14 sts).

Rnd 6: *sc in next 6 sts, 2 sc in next st" 2 times (16 sts).

Rnd 7: sc in each st around.

Rnd 8: *sc in next 6 sts, sc2tog* 2 times (14 sts).

Rnd 9: *sc in next 5 sts, sc2tog* 2 times (12 sts).

Rnd 10: *sc in next 4 sts, sc2tog* 2 times (10 sts).

Rnd 11: *sc in next 3 sts, sc2tog* 2 times (8 sts).

Sl st in next st. Fasten off with long tail.

SPOT (MAKE 3)

Each Spot is made in 2 sections.

Part A

With black yarn, make a magic ring, ch 1.

Rnd 1: 6 sc in ring, pull ring closed tight (6 sts).

Rnd 2: 2 sc in each st around. Place marker for beginning of rnd and move marker up as each rnd is completed (12 sts).

Rnd 3: *sc in next st, 2 sc in next st* 6 times (18 sts).

Rnd 4: *2 sc in next st, sc in next 2 sts* 6 times (24 sts).

Rnd 5: *sc in next 3 sts, 2 sc in next st* 6 times (30 sts).

Sl st in next st. Fasten off with long tail.

Part B

With black yarn, ch 2.

Row 1: 3 sc in 2nd ch from hook (3 sts).

Row 2: ch 1, turn, 2 sc in each st across (6 sts).

Row 3: ch 1, turn, *sc in next st, 2 sc in next st* 3 times (9 sts).

Row 4: ch 1, turn, *sc in next 2 sts, 2 sc in next st* 3 times (12 sts).

Fasten off with long tail. Place straight side of Part B anywhere against side of Part A and sew together.

HORN (MAKE 2)

With brown yarn, make a magic ring, ch 1.

Rnd 1: 4 sc in ring, pull ring closed tight (4 sts).

Rnd 2: sc in next 3 sts, 2 sc in next st. Place marker for beginning of rnd and move marker up as each rnd is completed (5 sts).

Rnd 3: sc in next 4 sts, 2 sc in next st (6 sts).

Rnd 4: sc in next 5 sts, 2 sc in next st (7 sts).

Rnd 5: sc in next 6 sts, 2 sc in next st (8 sts).

Fasten off with long tail.

ASSEMBLY

With a double strand of dark pink yarn, embroider 2 French knots on Snout. Mark position of Snout on Hat with disappearing ink marking pen and template (see page 79). Stuff Snout and sew to Hat. Sew Spots to Hat —1 on each side and 1 on back. Sew Ears, Horns and Eyes to Hat. Weave in ends. ♦

Monster

SUPPLIES

Worsted weight yarn in blue (approx. 100 yards) plus small amount of orange, yellow, red, white and black

Size H/8 (5 mm) crochet hook or size needed to obtain gauge

Disappearing ink marking pen

Fiberfill stuffing

Stitch marker

Yarn needle

GAUGE

7 rnds of sc = 3" diameter circle

HAT

With blue yarn, make a magic ring, ch 1.

Rnd 1: 6 sc in ring, pull ring closed tight (6 sts).

Rnd 2: 2 sc in each st around. Place marker for beginning of rnd and move marker up as each rnd is completed (12 sts).

Rnd 3: *sc in next st, 2 sc in next st* 6 times (18 sts).

Rnd 4: *sc in next 2 sts, 2 sc in next st* 6 times (24 sts).

Rnd 5: *sc in next 3 sts, 2 sc in next st* 6 times (30 sts).

Rnd 6: *sc in next 4 sts, 2 sc in next st* 6 times (36 sts).

Rnd 7: *sc in next 5 sts, 2 sc in next st* 6 times (42 sts).

Rnd 8: *sc in next 6 sts, 2 sc in next st* 6 times (48 sts).

Rnd 9: *sc in next 7 sts, 2 sc in next st* 6 times (54 sts).

• FOR SIZE SMALL:

Rnds 10-27: sc in each st around. Fasten off.

• FOR SIZE MEDIUM:

Rnd 10: *sc in next 8 sts, 2 sc in next st* 6 times (60 sts).

Rnds 11-30: sc in each st around. Fasten off.

• FOR SIZE LARGE:

Rnd 10: *sc in next 8 sts, 2 sc in next st* 6 times (60 sts).

Rnd 11: *sc in next 9 sts, 2 sc in next st* 6 times (66 sts).

Rnds 12-33: sc in each st around. Fasten off.

INNER EYE (MAKE 2)

With black yarn, make a magic ring, ch 1.

Rnd 1: 5 sc in ring, pull ring closed tight.

Sl st in next st. Fasten off with long tail.

OUTER EYE (MAKE 2)

With yellow yarn, make a magic ring, ch 1.

Rnd 1: 8 sc in ring, pull ring closed tight (8 sts).

Rnd 2a: 2 sc in next 3 sts (6 sts).

Point: ch 2 and sc in 2nd ch from hook, sc in next st.

Rnd 2b: 2 sc in next 3 sts (6 sts).

Point: ch 2 and sc in 2nd ch from hook, sc in next st.

Sl st in next st. Fasten off with long tail.

MOUTH

With red yarn, ch 14 loosely.

Row 1: sc in 2nd ch from hook and in each remaining ch across (13 sts).

Rows 2-4: ch 1, turn, sc in each st across (13 sts).

Fasten off with long tail.

TOOTH (MAKE 12)

With white yarn, embroider 6 pointy teeth across top and bottom of mouth making each tooth about 1/2 inch x 1/2 inch and wrapping sts around edge of mouth: Referring to

F E D C B

A

Tooth Guide

Tooth Guide, bring needle up at A, wrap around edge at B, up at A, wrap around edge at C, etc. to create a triangle. Weave in ends.

HORN (MAKE 2)

With orange yarn, make a magic ring, ch 1.

Rnd 1: 4 sc in ring, pull ring closed tight (4 sts).

Rnd 2: *sc in next st, 2 sc in next st* 2 times. Place marker for beginning of rnd and move marker up as each rnd is completed (6 sts).

Rnd 3: sc in each st around.

Rnd 4: *sc in next 2 sts, 2 sc in next st* 2 times (8 sts).

Rnd 5: sc in next st, sl st in next 2 sts, sc in next 5 sts (8 sts).

Rnd 6: sc in next st, sl st in next 2 sts, 2 sc in next st, sc in next 3 sts, 2 sc in next st (10 sts).

Rnd 7: sc in next st, sl st in next 2 sts, sc in next 7 sts (10 sts).

Rnd 8: *sc in next 4 sts, 2 sc in next st* 2 times (12 sts).

Rnd 9: sc in each st around.

Rnd 10: *sc in next 5 sts, 2 sc in next st* 2 times (14 sts).

Rnd 11: sc in each st around.

Rnd 12: *sc in next 6 sts, 2 sc in next st* 2 times (16 sts).

Sl st in next st. Fasten off with long tail.

ASSEMBLY

Mark position of Horns on Hat with disappearing ink marking pen and circle templates (see page 80). Stuff Horns and sew to Hat. Sew Inner Eyes to Outer Eyes. Sew Eyes and Mouth in place. ♦

Bunny

SUPPLIES

Worsted weight yarn in beige (approx. 125 yards) plus small amount of pink and black

Size H/8 (5 mm) crochet hook or size needed to obtain gauge

Disappearing ink marking pen

Hole punch

Stitch marker

Yarn needle

GAUGE

7 rnds of sc = 3" diameter circle

HAT

With beige yarn, make a magic ring, ch 1.

Rnd 1: 6 sc in ring, pull ring closed tight (6 sts).

Rnd 2: 2 sc in each st around. Place marker for beginning of rnd and move marker up as each rnd is completed (12 sts).

Rnd 3: *sc in next st, 2 sc in next st* 6 times (18 sts).

Rnd 4: *sc in next 2 sts, 2 sc in next st* 6 times (24 sts).

Rnd 5: *sc in next 3 sts, 2 sc in next st* 6 times (30 sts).

Rnd 6: *sc in next 4 sts, 2 sc in next st* 6 times (36 sts).

Rnd 7: *sc in next 5 sts, 2 sc in next st* 6 times (42 sts).

Rnd 8: *sc in next 6 sts, 2 sc in next st* 6 times (48 sts).

Rnd 9: *sc in next 7 sts, 2 sc in next st* 6 times (54 sts).

• FOR SIZE SMALL:

Rnds 10-27: sc in each st around. Fasten off.

• FOR SIZE MEDIUM:

Rnd 10: *sc in next 8 sts, 2 sc in next st* 6 times (60 sts).

Rnds 11-30: sc in each st around. Fasten off.

• FOR SIZE LARGE:

Rnd 10: *sc in next 8 sts, 2 sc in next st* 6 times (60 sts).

Rnd 11: *sc in next 9 sts, 2 sc in next st* 6 times (66 sts).

Rnds 12-33: sc in each st around. Fasten off.

EAR (MAKE 2)

With beige yarn, make a magic ring, ch 1.

Rnd 1: 6 sc in ring, pull ring closed tight (6 sts).

Rnd 2: 2 sc in each st around. Place marker for beginning of rnd and move marker up as each rnd is completed (12 sts).

Rnd 3: *sc in next st, 2 sc in next st* 6 times (18 sts).

Rnds 4-8: sc in each st around.

Rnd 9: *sc in next 4 sts, sc2tog* 3 times (15 sts).

Rnds 10-11: sc in each st around.

Rnd 12: *sc in next 3 sts, sc2tog* 3 times (12 sts).

Rnds 13-15: sc in each st around.

Fasten off with long tail.

EYE (MAKE 2)

With black yarn, make a magic ring, ch 1.

Rnd 1: 5 sc in ring, pull ring closed tight (5 sts).

Sl st in next st. Fasten off with long tail.

NOSE

With pink yarn, make a magic ring, ch 1.

Rnd 1: 4 sc in ring, pull ring closed tight (4 sts).

Sl st in next st. Fasten off with long tail.

MOUTH

To mark mouth, trace template onto office paper (see page 79). Punch holes in corners and tips.

Place template in position on Hat and dot with disappearing ink into the holes. Remove paper and connect dots.

With pink yarn, sew along outline with running stitch. Now sew in opposite direction to fill in the spaces, inserting needle through a bit of the stitches on either side to avoid gaps.

TIE

With pink yarn, make a 14-inch chain. Fasten off. Weave in ends.

ASSEMBLY

Sew Nose and Eyes to Hat. Shape open end of Ears into a circle and mark placement on Hat with disappearing ink marking pen and circle templates (see page 80). Sew Ears to Hat. *Note: Do not flatten open end of Ears. Keeping open end circular will result in Ears that stand up.* Fasten Tie in a bow around one Ear. Weave in ends. ♦

Bee

SUPPLIES

Worsted weight yarn in yellow (approx. 50 yards) and black (approx. 50 yards) plus small amount of white and orange

Size H/8 (5 mm) crochet hook or size needed to obtain gauge

Stitch marker

Yarn needle

GAUGE

7 rnds of sc = 3" diameter circle

HAT

With yellow yarn, make a magic ring, ch 1.

Rnd 1: 6 sc in ring, pull ring closed tight (6 sts).

Rnd 2: 2 sc in each st around. Place marker for beginning of rnd and move marker up as each rnd is completed (12 sts).

Rnd 3: *sc in next st, 2 sc in next st* 6 times (18 sts).

Rnd 4: *sc in next 2 sts, 2 sc in next st* 6 times (24 sts).

Rnd 5: *sc in next 3 sts, 2 sc in next st* 6 times (30 sts).

Rnd 6: *sc in next 4 sts, 2 sc in next st* 6 times (36 sts).

Rnd 7: *sc in next 5 sts, 2 sc in next st* 6 times (42 sts).

Rnd 8: *sc in next 6 sts, 2 sc in next st* 6 times (48 sts).

Rnd 9: *sc in next 7 sts, 2 sc in next st* 6 times (54 sts).

• FOR SIZE SMALL:

Fasten on with black yarn.

Rnds 10-27: sc in each st around alternating 2 rnds of black with 2 rnds of yellow; change to alternate color in last st of every other rnd. Fasten off.

• FOR SIZE MEDIUM:

Rnd 10: *sc in next 8 sts, 2 sc in next st* 6 times; change to black yarn in last st (60 sts).

Rnds 11-30: sc in each st around alternating 2 rnds of black with 2 rnds of yellow; change to alternate color in last st of every other rnd. Fasten off.

• FOR SIZE LARGE:

Rnd 10: *sc in next 8 sts, 2 sc in next st* 6 times (60 sts).

Rnd 11: *sc in next 9 sts, 2 sc in next st* 6 times; change to black yarn in last st (66 sts).

Rnds 12-33: sc in each st around alternating 2 rnds of black with 2 rnds of yellow; change to alternate color in last st of every other rnd. Fasten off.

INNER EYE (MAKE 2)

With black yarn, make a magic ring, ch 1.

Rnd 1: 4 sc in ring, pull ring closed tight (4 sts).

Sl st in next st. Fasten off with long tail.

OUTER EYE (MAKE 2)

With white yarn, make a magic ring, ch 1.

Rnd 1: 6 sc in ring, pull ring closed tight (6 sts).

Rnd 2: 2 sc in each st around. Place marker for beginning of rnd and move marker up as each rnd is completed (12 sts).

Rnd 3: *sc in next st, 2 sc in next st* 6 times (18 sts).

Sl st in next st. Fasten off with long tail.

ANTENNA (MAKE 2)

With black yarn, make a magic ring, ch 1.

Rnd 1: 6 sc in ring, pull ring closed tight (6 sts).

Rnd 2: sc in each st around.

Rnd 3: *sc in next st, sc2tog* 2 times (4 sts).

Rnds 4-?: sc in each st around until antenna measures 2" long. Fasten off with long tail. Thread yarn needle with long tail and run yarn up and down through length of antenna 2 times to stiffen.

MOUTH

With orange yarn, ch 7.

Row 1: starting in 2nd ch from hook, sc2tog, sc in next 2 sts, sc2tog (4 sts).

Row 2: ch 1, turn, sc2tog twice (2 sts).

Row 3: ch 1, turn, sc2tog (1 st).

Fasten off with long tail.

ASSEMBLY

Sew Inner Eyes to Outer Eyes. Sew Eyes, Mouth and Antennae to Hat. Weave in ends. ♦

Chicken

SUPPLIES

Worsted weight yarn in white (approx. 100 yards) plus small amount of red, yellow and black

Size H/8 (5 mm) crochet hook or size needed to obtain gauge

Small piece of cardboard

Stitch marker

Yarn needle

GAUGE

7 rnds of sc = 3" diameter circle

HAT

With white yarn, make a magic ring, ch 1.

Rnd 1: 6 sc in ring, pull ring closed tight (6 sts).

Rnd 2: 2 sc in each st around. Place marker for beginning of rnd and move marker up as each rnd is completed (12 sts).

Rnd 3: *sc in next st, 2 sc in next st* 6 times (18 sts).

Rnd 4: *sc in next 2 sts, 2 sc in next st* 6 times (24 sts).

Rnd 5: *sc in next 3 sts, 2 sc in next st* 6 times (30 sts).

Rnd 6: *sc in next 4 sts, 2 sc in next st* 6 times (36 sts).

Rnd 7: *sc in next 5 sts, 2 sc in next st* 6 times (42 sts).

Rnd 8: *sc in next 6 sts, 2 sc in next st* 6 times (48 sts).

Rnd 9: *sc in next 7 sts, 2 sc in next st* 6 times (54 sts).

• FOR SIZE SMALL:

Rnds 10-27: sc in each st around. Fasten off.

• FOR SIZE MEDIUM:

Rnd 10: *sc in next 8 sts, 2 sc in next st* 6 times (60 sts).

Rnds 11-30: sc in each st around. Fasten off.

• FOR SIZE LARGE:

Rnd 10: *sc in next 8 sts, 2 sc in next st* 6 times (60 sts).

Rnd 11: *sc in next 9 sts, 2 sc in next st* 6 times (66 sts).

Rnds 12-33: sc in each st around. Fasten off.

COMB

Cut a rectangle of cardboard measuring 2" x 6". Wrap red yarn widthwise around the cardboard 75 times. Carefully slide yarn off cardboard. Using a scrap of yarn, tie bundle together tightly around the middle. Wrap tails of tie to opposite side and tie again. Cut loops open. (See Pom Poms, page 15.) Fluff pom pom and trim ends into a nice round shape.

EYE (MAKE 2)

With black yarn, make a magic ring, ch 1.

Rnd 1: 6 sc in ring, pull ring closed tight (6 sts).

Sl st in next st. Fasten off with long tail.

BEAK (MAKE 2)

With yellow yarn, make a magic ring, ch 1.

Rnd 1: 4 sc in ring, pull ring closed tight (4 sts).

Rnd 2: sc in next 3 sts, 2 sc in next st. Place marker for beginning of rnd and move marker up as each rnd is completed (5 sts).

Rnd 3: sc in next 4 sts, 2 sc in next st (6 sts).

Rnd 4: sc in next 5 sts, 2 sc in next st (7 sts).

Rnd 5: sc in next 6 sts, 2 sc in next st (8 sts).

Rnd 6: sc in next 7 sts, 2 sc in next st (9 sts).

Fasten off with long tail.

ASSEMBLY

Flatten and stack Beak pieces. Sew the two adjoining edges together to make a hinge. Sew Beak and Eyes to front of Hat. Tie Comb to top of Hat. Weave in ends. ♦

Octopus

SUPPLIES

Worsted weight yarn in aqua (approx. 140 yards) plus small amount of black and white

Size H/8 (5 mm) crochet hook or size needed to obtain gauge

Stitch marker

Yarn needle

GAUGE

7 rnds of sc = 3" diameter circle

HAT

With aqua yarn, make a magic ring, ch 1.

Rnd 1: 6 sc in ring, pull ring closed tight (6 sts).

Rnd 2: 2 sc in each st around. Place marker for beginning of rnd and move marker up as each rnd is completed (12 sts).

Rnd 3: *sc in next st, 2 sc in next st* 6 times (18 sts).

Rnd 4: *sc in next 2 sts, 2 sc in next st* 6 times (24 sts).

Rnd 5: *sc in next 3 sts, 2 sc in next st* 6 times (30 sts).

Rnd 6: *sc in next 4 sts, 2 sc in next st* 6 times (36 sts).

Rnd 7: *sc in next 5 sts, 2 sc in next st* 6 times (42 sts).

Rnd 8: *sc in next 6 sts, 2 sc in next st* 6 times (48 sts).

Rnd 9: *sc in next 7 sts, 2 sc in next st* 6 times (54 sts).

• FOR SIZE SMALL:

Rnds 10-27: sc in each st around. Fasten off.

• FOR SIZE MEDIUM:

Rnd 10: *sc in next 8 sts, 2 sc in next st* 6 times (60 sts).

Rnds 11-30: sc in each st around. Fasten off.

• FOR SIZE LARGE:

Rnd 10: *sc in next 8 sts, 2 sc in next st* 6 times (60 sts).

Rnd 11: *sc in next 9 sts, 2 sc in next st* 6 times (66 sts).

Rnds 12-33: sc in each st around. Fasten off.

ARM (MAKE 8)

With aqua yarn, ch 31 loosely.

Row 1: sc in 2nd ch from hook and in each remaining ch across (30 sts).

Rows 2-3: ch 1, turn, sc in each st across (30 sts).

Fasten off with long tail.

INNER EYE (MAKE 2)

With black yarn, make a magic ring, ch 1.

Rnd 1: 6 sc in ring, pull ring closed tight (6 sts).

Sl st in next st. Fasten off with long tail.

OUTER EYE (MAKE 2)

With white yarn, make a magic ring, ch 1.

Rnd 1: 6 sc in ring, pull ring closed tight (6 sts).

Rnd 2: 2 sc in each st around. Place marker for beginning of rnd and move marker up as each rnd is completed (12 sts).

Rnd 3: *sc in next st, 2 sc in next st* 6 times (18 sts).

Sl st in next st. Fasten off with long tail.

ASSEMBLY

Sew Inner Eyes to Outer Eyes. Sew Eyes to Hat. Sew Arms to lower edge of Hat—around back and sides. Weave in ends. ♦

Snow Leopard

SUPPLIES

Worsted weight yarn in pale gray (approx. 110 yards) plus small amount of black, peach and white

Size H/8 (5 mm) crochet hook or size needed to obtain gauge

Polyester felt in olive green and black

Thread in olive green and black

Disappearing ink marking pen

Stitch marker

Yarn needle

GAUGE

7 rnds of sc = 3" diameter circle

HAT

With pale gray yarn, make a magic ring, ch 1.

Rnd 1: 6 sc in ring, pull ring closed tight (6 sts).

Rnd 2: 2 sc in each st around. Place marker for beginning of rnd and move marker up as each rnd is completed (12 sts).

Rnd 3: *sc in next st, 2 sc in next st* 6 times (18 sts).

Rnd 4: *sc in next 2 sts, 2 sc in next st* 6 times (24 sts).

Rnd 5: *sc in next 3 sts, 2 sc in next st* 6 times (30 sts).

Rnd 6: *sc in next 4 sts, 2 sc in next st* 6 times (36 sts).

Rnd 7: *sc in next 5 sts, 2 sc in next st* 6 times (42 sts).

Rnd 8: *sc in next 6 sts, 2 sc in next st* 6 times (48 sts).

Rnd 9: *sc in next 7 sts, 2 sc in next st* 6 times (54 sts).

• **FOR SIZE SMALL:**

Rnds 10-27: sc in each st around. Fasten off.

• **FOR SIZE MEDIUM:**

Rnd 10: *sc in next 8 sts, 2 sc in next st* 6 times (60 sts).

Rnds 11-30: sc in each st around. Fasten off.

• **FOR SIZE LARGE:**

Rnd 10: *sc in next 8 sts, 2 sc in next st* 6 times (60 sts).

Rnd 11: *sc in next 9 sts, 2 sc in next st* 6 times (66 sts).

Rnds 12-33: sc in each st around. Fasten off.

INNER EYE (MAKE 2)

Cut a 5/8" circle of olive green felt and a 3/8" circle of black felt (see templates, page 80). Stack black circle on olive green circle and whip stitch in place.

OUTER EYE (MAKE 2)

With black yarn, make a magic ring, ch 1.

Rnd 1: 8 sc in ring, pull ring closed tight (8 sts).

Rnd 2a: 2 sc in next 3 sts (6 sts).

Point: ch 2 and sc in 2nd ch from hook, sc in next st.

Rnd 2b: 2 sc in next 3 sts (6 sts).

Point: ch 2 and sc in 2nd ch from hook, sc in next st.

Sl st in next st. Fasten off with long tail.

EAR (MAKE 2)

With pale gray yarn, make a magic ring, ch 1.

Rnd 1: 6 sc in ring, pull ring closed tight (6 sts).

Rnd 2: 2 sc in each st around. Place marker for beginning of rnd and move marker up as each rnd is completed (12 sts).

Rnd 3: *sc in next st, 2 sc in next st* 6 times (18 sts).

Rnds 4-7: sc in each st around.

Fasten off with long tail.

SNOUT

With pale gray yarn, ch 9 loosely.

Row 1: sc in 2nd ch from hook and in each remaining ch across (8 sts).

Rows 2-8: ch 1, turn, sc in each st across (8 sts).

Row 9: ch 1, turn, sc2tog, sc in next 4 sts, sc2tog (6 sts).

Row 10: ch 1, turn, sc2tog, sc in next 2 sts, sc2tog (4 sts).

Row 11: ch 1, turn, sc2tog twice (2 sts).

Row 12: ch 1, turn, sc2tog (1 st).

Fasten off with long tail.

NOSE

With peach yarn, ch 9 loosely.

Row 1: starting in 2nd ch from hook, sc2tog, sc in next 4 sts, sc2tog (6 sts).

Row 2: ch 1, turn, sc2tog, sc in next 2 sts, sc2tog (4 sts).

Row 3: ch 1, turn, sc2tog twice (2 sts).

Row 4: ch 1, turn, sc2tog (1 st).

Fasten off with long tail.

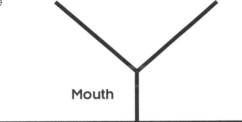

Mouth

ASSEMBLY

Flatten Ears and sew to Hat. Sew Snout to Hat. Sew Nose to Snout. Sew Inner Eyes to Outer Eyes. Sew Eyes to Hat. Using a double strand of black yarn, embroider mouth (see diagram). Using a single strand of white yarn, embroider whiskers. With disappearing ink marking pen, draw irregular circles and ovals on Hat for leopard's spots. Using black yarn, outline the spots with chain stitch embroidery (see page 15). Note: *I like to embroider the spots with a long strand of yarn, weaving through the underside from one spot to the next.* Weave in ends. ♦

Bear

SUPPLIES

Worsted weight yarn in tan (approx. 120 yards) plus small amount of black and red

Size H/8 (5 mm) crochet hook or size needed to obtain gauge

Disappearing ink marking pen

Fiberfill stuffing

Stitch marker

Yarn needle

GAUGE

7 rnds of sc = 3" diameter circle

HAT

With tan yarn, make a magic ring, ch 1.

Rnd 1: 6 sc in ring, pull ring closed tight (6 sts).

Rnd 2: 2 sc in each st around. Place marker for beginning of rnd and move marker up as each rnd is completed (12 sts).

Rnd 3: *sc in next st, 2 sc in next st* 6 times (18 sts).

Rnd 4: *sc in next 2 sts, 2 sc in next st* 6 times (24 sts).

Rnd 5: *sc in next 3 sts, 2 sc in next st* 6 times (30 sts).

Rnd 6: *sc in next 4 sts, 2 sc in next st* 6 times (36 sts).

Rnd 7: *sc in next 5 sts, 2 sc in next st* 6 times (42 sts).

Rnd 8: *sc in next 6 sts, 2 sc in next st* 6 times (48 sts).

Rnd 9: *sc in next 7 sts, 2 sc in next st* 6 times (54 sts).

• FOR SIZE SMALL:

Rnds 10-27: sc in each st around. Fasten off.

• FOR SIZE MEDIUM:

Rnd 10: *sc in next 8 sts, 2 sc in next st* 6 times (60 sts).

Rnds 11-30: sc in each st around. Fasten off.

• FOR SIZE LARGE:

Rnd 10: *sc in next 8 sts, 2 sc in next st* 6 times (60 sts).

Rnd 11: *sc in next 9 sts, 2 sc in next st* 6 times (66 sts).

Rnds 12-33: sc in each st around. Fasten off.

EYE (MAKE 2)

With black yarn, make a magic ring, ch 1.

Rnd 1: 6 sc in ring, pull ring closed tight (6 sts).

Sl st in next st. Fasten off with long tail.

NOSE

With black yarn, make a magic ring, ch 1.

Rnd 1: 5 sc in ring, pull ring closed tight (5 sts).

Sl st in next st. Fasten off with long tail.

SNOUT

With tan yarn, make a magic ring, ch 1.

Rnd 1: 6 sc in ring, pull ring closed tight (6 sts).

Rnd 2: 2 sc in each st around. Place marker for beginning of rnd and move marker up as each rnd is completed (12 sts).

Rnd 3: sc in each st around.

Rnd 4: *sc in next st, 2 sc in next st* 6 times (18 sts).

Rnd 5: sc in each st around.

Rnd 6: *sc in next 2 sts, 2 sc in next st* 6 times (24 sts).

Rnd 7: sc in each st around.

Sl st in next st. Fasten off with long tail.

EAR (MAKE 2)

With tan yarn, make a magic ring, ch 1.

Rnd 1: 6 sc in ring, pull ring closed tight (6 sts).

Rnd 2: 2 sc in each st around. Place marker for beginning of rnd and move marker up as each rnd is completed (12 sts).

Rnd 3: *sc in next st, 2 sc in next st* 6 times (18 sts).

Rnds 4-7: sc in each st around.

Fasten off with long tail.

ASSEMBLY

Flatten Ears and sew to top of Hat. Sew Nose to center of Snout. With red yarn, embroider mouth on Snout with one straight stitch. Mark position of Snout on Hat with disappearing ink marking pen and circle template (see page 80). Stuff Snout and sew in place. Sew Eyes to Hat. Weave in ends. ♦

Tiger

SUPPLIES

Worsted weight yarn in orange (approx. 80 yards) and black (approx. 25 yards) plus small amount of white

Size H/8 (5 mm) crochet hook or size needed to obtain gauge

Stitch marker

Yarn needle

GAUGE

7 rnds of sc = 3" diameter circle

HAT

Make Hat by alternating 3 rnds of orange yarn with 1 rnd, then 2 rnds, of black yarn throughout. (Refer to project photo, page 76.) Change to alternate color in last st of previous rnd. For example, to work Rnd 4 in black, change to black yarn in last st of Rnd 3.

With orange yarn, make a magic ring, ch 1.

Rnd 1: 6 sc in ring, pull ring closed tight (6 sts).

Rnd 2: 2 sc in each st around. Place marker for beginning of rnd and move marker up as each rnd is completed (12 sts).

Rnd 3: *sc in next st, 2 sc in next st* 6 times (18 sts).

Rnd 4: *sc in next 2 sts, 2 sc in next st* 6 times (24 sts).

Rnd 5: *sc in next 3 sts, 2 sc in next st* 6 times (30 sts).

Rnd 6: *sc in next 4 sts, 2 sc in next st* 6 times (36 sts).

Rnd 7: *sc in next 5 sts, 2 sc in next st* 6 times (42 sts).

Rnd 8: *sc in next 6 sts, 2 sc in next st* 6 times (48 sts).

Rnd 9: *sc in next 7 sts, 2 sc in next st* 6 times (54 sts).

• FOR SIZE SMALL:

Rnds 10-27: sc in each st around. Fasten off.

• FOR SIZE MEDIUM:

Rnd 10: *sc in next 8 sts, 2 sc in next st* 6 times (60 sts).

Rnds 11-30: sc in each st around. Fasten off.

• FOR SIZE LARGE:

Rnd 10: *sc in next 8 sts, 2 sc in next st* 6 times (60 sts).

Rnd 11: *sc in next 9 sts, 2 sc in next st* 6 times (66 sts).

Rnds 12-33: sc in each st around. Fasten off.

INNER EYE (MAKE 2)

With black yarn, make a magic ring, ch 1.

Rnd 1: 6 sc in ring, pull ring closed tight (6 sts).

Sl st in next st. Fasten off with long tail.

OUTER EYE (MAKE 2)

With white yarn, make a magic ring, ch 1.

Rnd 1: 6 sc in ring, pull ring closed tight (6 sts).

Rnd 2: 2 sc in each st around. Place marker for beginning of rnd and move marker up as each rnd is completed (12 sts).

Rnd 3: *sc in next st, 2 sc in next st* 6 times (18 sts).

Sl st in next st. Fasten off with long tail.

SNOUT

With white yarn, make a magic ring, ch 1.

Rnd 1: 6 sc in ring, pull ring closed tight (6 sts).

Rnd 2: 2 sc in each st around. Place marker for beginning of rnd and move marker up as each rnd is completed (12 sts).

Rnd 3: *sc in next st, 2 sc in next st* 6 times (18 sts).

Rnd 4: *2 sc in next st, sc in next 2 sts* 6 times (24 sts).

Rnd 5: *sc in next 3 sts, 2 sc in next st* 6 times (30 sts).

Sl st in next st. Fasten off with long tail.

NOSE

With black yarn, make a magic ring, ch 1.

Rnd 1: 5 sc in ring, pull ring closed tight (5 sts).

Sl st in next st. Fasten off with long tail.

EAR (MAKE 2)

With orange yarn, make a magic ring, ch 1.

Rnd 1: 6 sc in ring, pull ring closed tight (6 sts).

Rnd 2: 2 sc in each st around. Place marker for beginning of rnd and move marker up as each rnd is completed (12 sts).

Rnd 3: *sc in next st, 2 sc in next st* 6 times (18 sts).

Rnds 4-7: sc in each st around.

Fasten off with long tail.

ASSEMBLY

Sew Ears to Hat. Pull top and bottom of Snout to make an oval shape. Sew Nose to Snout and embroider mouth with straight stitches (see diagram). Sew Snout to Hat. Sew Inner Eyes to Outer Eyes. Sew Eyes to Hat. Weave in ends. ◆

Mouth

Templates

Copy or trace the templates at 100 percent.

Lion

snout, page 29

**Lion
Snout Template**

To mark Snout placement,
copy and cut out Template.
Pin in position to Hat.
Trace with Disappearing Ink
Marking Pen.

Sock Monkey

snout, page 51

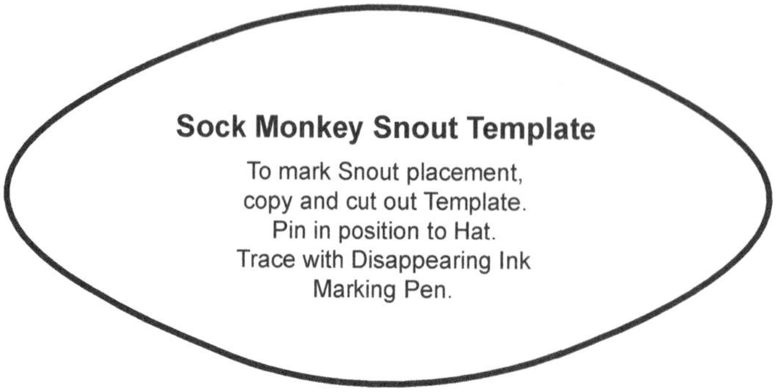

Sock Monkey Snout Template

To mark Snout placement,
copy and cut out Template.
Pin in position to Hat.
Trace with Disappearing Ink
Marking Pen.

Frog

mouth, page 32

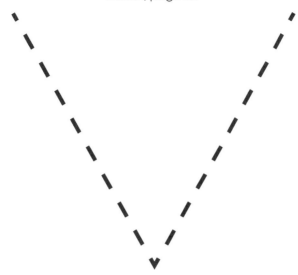

Cow

snout, page 54

**Cow
Snout Template**

To mark Snout placement,
copy and cut out Template.
Pin in position to Hat.
Trace with Disappearing Ink
Marking Pen.

Bunny

mouth, page 59

For felt eyes, select specified size, cut around pattern leaving excess paper, tape in position to felt with Scotch Removable Double Sided Tape and cut around outside of black line. Remove pattern. If using template to mark placement of auxiliary pieces, cut a circle that matches the open end of your piece, pin in position to hat and trace with disappearing ink marking pen. Remove pattern and pin amigurumi piece over outline to sew in place.

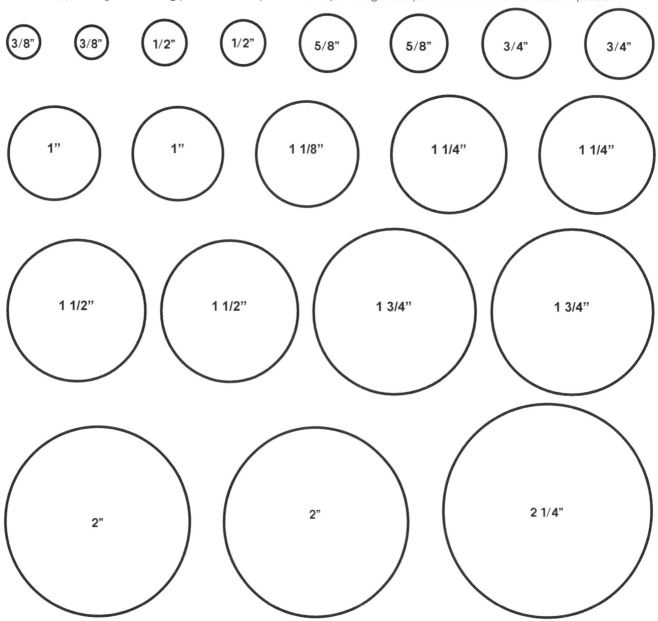

ReSourceS

YARN

Caron Yarn
caron.com
Simply Soft

Lion Brand
lionbrand.com
Vanna's Choice
Cotton Ease

Red Heart
redheart.com
Soft Yarn

Hobby Lobby
shop.hobbylobby.com
I Love This Yarn

Michaels
michaels.com
Loops & Threads *Impeccable*
Loops & Threads *Soft & Shiny*

Joann Fabric and Craft Stores
joann.com
Caron *Simply Soft*
Lion Brand *Vanna's Choice*
Lion Brand *Cotton Ease*
Red Heart *Soft Yarn*

NOTIONS

Joann Fabric and Craft Stores
joann.com
Clover Soft Touch Crochet Hook
Disappearing ink marking pen
Jumbo tapestry needles
Locking stitch markers
Fiberfill stuffing
Knitting counter
Scotch Removable Double
Sided Tape

**General Specialty Tools
& Instruments**
generaltools.com
Arch punches

FELT

Joann Fabric and Craft Stores
joann.com
Rainbow Classic Felt 9" x 12"

The Hobby Co. of San Francisco
hobbycosf.com
Rainbow Classic Felt 9" x 12"

VIDEO TUTORIALS

You Tube !
youtube.com
Search on the name of the stitch or technique you want to learn.

Pinterest
pinterest.com/LindalooEnt/
Visit my Pinterest page to view video tutorials for the stitches and techniques used in this book. Look for the boards named "Amigurumi Tutorials" and "Embroidery Tutorials".

Featured Yarn

The following yarns were used for these amigurumi animal hats.

Owl

Caron "Simply Soft"

Color: Lavender Blue, #9756

Color: Pistachio, #0003

Color: Blue Mint, #9608

Color: Sunshine #9755

Color: White, #9701

Color: Black, #9727

Cat

Lion Brand "Vanna's Choice"

Color: Silver Gray, #149

Color: Silver Heather, #405

Caron "Simply Soft"

Color: Coconut, #9601

Color: Black, #9727

Color: Strawberry, #0015

Sheep

Loops & Threads "Impeccable"

Color: Aran, #01008

Caron "Simply Soft"

Color: Black, #9727

Lion

Lion Brand "Cotton-Ease"

Color: Maize, #186

Lion Brand "Homespun Thick & Quick"

Color: Natural Stripes, #206

Caron "Simply Soft"

Color: Black, #9727

Frog

Lion Brand "Vanna's Choice"

Color: Dusty Green #173

Caron "Simply Soft"

Color: Coconut, #9601

Color: Watermelon, #9604

Red Heart "Soft Yarn"

Color: Berry, #9779

Panda

Caron "Simply Soft"

Color: Coconut, #9601

Color: Black, #9727

Color: Watermelon, #9604

Stegosaurus

Caron "Simply Soft"

Color: Berry Blue, #9609

Color: Coconut, #9601

Color: Black, #9727

Lion Brand "Vanna's Choice"

Color: Honey #130

Duck

Caron "Simply Soft"

Color: Lemonade, #9776

Color: Coconut, #9601

Color: Mango, #9605

Dog

Lion Brand "Vanna's Choice"

Color: Oatmeal, #400

Color: Barley, #403

Caron "Simply Soft"

Color: Black, #9727

Color: Strawberry, #0015

Pig

Caron "Simply Soft"

Color: Strawberry, #0015

Color: Black, #9727

Sock Monkey

Caron "Simply Soft"

> Color: Grey Heather, #9742
>
> Color: Off White, #9702
>
> Color: Autumn Red, #9730
>
> Color: Black, #9727

Cow

Caron "Simply Soft"

> Color: Coconut, #9601
>
> Color: Black, #9727
>
> Color: Nutmeg, #0013
>
> Color: Soft Pink, #9719
>
> Color: Watermelon, #9604

Monster

Caron "Simply Soft"

> Color: Country Blue, #9710
>
> Color: Coconut, #9601
>
> Color: Black, #9727
>
> Color: Lemonade, #9776
>
> Color: Autumn Red, #9730

Red Heart "Soft Yarn"

> Color: Tangerine, #4422

Bunny

Caron "Simply Soft"

> Color: Bone, #9703
>
> Color: Watermelon, #9604
>
> Color: Black, #9727

Bee

Caron "Simply Soft"

> Color: Sunshine, #9755
>
> Color: Black, #9727
>
> Color: White, #9701
>
> Color: Neon Orange, #9774

Chicken

Caron "Simply Soft"

> Color: Coconut, #9601
>
> Color: Red, #9729
>
> Color: Lemonade, #9776
>
> Color: Black, #9727

Octopus

Caron "Simply Soft"

> Color: Aqua Mist, #0007
>
> Color: Coconut, #9601
>
> Color: Black, #9727

Snow Leopard

Lion Brand "Vanna's Choice"

> Color: Linen, #099

Caron "Simply Soft"

> Color: Black, #9727
>
> Color: Coconut, #9601

Hobby Lobby "I Love This Yarn"

> Color: Peach, #458760

Bear

Red Heart "Soft Yarn"

> Color: Wheat, #9388

Caron "Simply Soft"

> Color: Red, #9729
>
> Color: Black, #9727

Tiger

Caron "Simply Soft"

> Color: Pumpkin, #9765
>
> Color: Black, #9727
>
> Color: Coconut, #9601

Yarn Care Symbols

Use this chart to interpret the universal care symbols on yarn labels. If a washing symbol includes a number in the wash tub, that indicates the maximum wash temperature (degrees Celsius). Drycleaning symbols may contain additional letters or lines. Take dryclean items to a professional drycleaner.

WASHING INSTRUCTIONS

 Machine Wash, COLD

 Machine Wash, COLD Perma Press

 Machine Wash, COLD Gentle Cycle

 Hand Wash

 Machine Wash, WARM

 Machine Wash, WARM Perma Press

 Machine Wash, WARM Gentle Cycle

 Do Not Wash

 Machine Wash, HOT

 Machine Wash, HOT Perma Press

 Machine Wash, HOT Gentle Cycle

BLEACHING INSTRUCTIONS

Bleach as needed
Any bleach may be safely used

Non-chlorine Bleach as needed
Use only a color-safe bleach

 Do Not Bleach

DRYING INSTRUCTIONS

 Tumble Dry, NO HEAT

 Tumble Dry, Perma Press, NO HEAT

 Tumble Dry, Gentle Cycle, NO HEAT

 Do Not Tumble Dry

 Tumble Dry, LOW HEAT

 Tumble Dry, Perma Press, LOW HEAT

 Tumble Dry, Gentle Cycle, LOW HEAT

 Line Dry

 Tumble Dry, MEDIUM

Tumble Dry, Perma Press, MEDIUM

Tumble Dry, Gentle Cycle, MEDIUM

 Drip Dry

 Tumble Dry, HIGH

Dry Flat

IRONING INSTRUCTIONS

Iron, Steam or Dry, with LOW HEAT

Iron, Steam or Dry, with MEDIUM HEAT

Iron, Steam or Dry, with HIGH HEAT

 Do Not Iron with Steam

 Do Not Iron

DRYCLEANING INSTRUCTIONS

Dry Clean

 Do Not Dry Clean

Other books by
Linda Wright

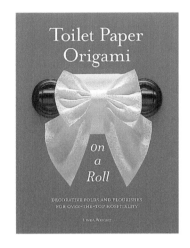

LINDA WRIGHT is the author of the bestselling *Toilet Paper Origami* and its companion book, *Toilet Paper Origami On a Roll*, as well as the innovative *Toilet Paper Crafts* and whimsical *Amigurumi Toilet Paper Covers*. To learn more about these fun-filled books, visit:

tporigami.com

and

pinterest.com/LindalooEnt/

Notes

CPSIA information can be obtained at www.ICGtesting.com
Printed in the USA
LVOW01s1546011214

416495LV00037B/323/P

9 780980 092370